Treasures from the Original Vol. III:

Studies in 2 Timothy

DR. HAROLD J. BERRY

Originally published as *Gems from the Original Vol. II: Studies in II Timothy.*

Gems from the Original Vol. II was published by The Good News Broadcasting Association, Inc. © 1975.

Unless otherwise identified, all Scripture quotations in this publication are taken from the *New American Standard Bible,* © 1960, 1962, 1963, 1968, 1971, 1972, 1973, 1975, 1977, 1995 by the Lockman Foundation and are used by permission.

Loved (5.5x8.5) Self-Publishing Template © 2017 Renee Fisher [https://www.reneefisher.com]

Cover Design: © Nelly Murariu at PixBeeDesign.com

ISBN-10: 0-578-66583-2
ISBN-13: 978-0-578-66583-2

Dedication

To Renee Fisher

Having written for publication for over 50 years, I have regretted that many items previously published were no longer available. This is always sad to see for a writer who pours his heart and soul into what he has produced. It is even sadder when one has written to explain the Scriptures, the written Word of God, and that is no longer available to teach others and lead unbelievers to the Lord.

I needed someone to work on my dreams, and then along comes Renee Fisher, the dream defender. I knew her grandparents when I was on staff at Back to the Bible in Lincoln, Nebraska. I also know her parents and it was through them that I saw that their daughter was a self-publisher. The rest is history. This is the fourth book she has helped me publish.

Renee is a talented, gracious Christ-follower and it is a pleasure to work with her. She is certainly a vessel of honor as mentioned in 2 Timothy 2:20.

Contents

Foreword

WE ALL LOOK to teachers who have the ability to explain God's Word. My friend, Harold Berry, has been doing that for years as a college professor, writer and speaker. God has given him the ability to understand the New Testament Greek language and communicate it in a way that will inform, enlighten and educate you.

He draws on his knowledge of the Greek language, his love for God's Word, and ability to share it in a way that will give you instruction into the biblical author's thinking. The Book of 2 Timothy is going to come alive for you without adding to your questions.

Harold's books have proven to be a great blessing to me personally and have been a source of spiritual enrichment for my people. I would recommend you add this book to your library and share it with friends who can benefit from a practical study in 2 Timothy.

With Loving Appreciation,

Pastor Paul Pletcher, ThM
Interim Pastor Ministries
Anderson, Indiana

Chapter 1 –
Background of 2
Timothy

THE FIRST MENTION of Timothy occurs in Acts 16:1. The Apostle Paul was on his second missionary journey, and when he went to Derbe and Lystra, "a disciple was there, named Timothy, the son of a Jewish woman who was a believer, but his father was a Greek" (v. 1).

It is possible that Timothy became a believer when Paul was at Derbe and Lystra during his first missionary journey. On that journey Paul was stoned by the people at Lystra, and Timothy might have realized then the need to receive Jesus Christ as his personal Savior. The apostle later referred to Timothy as "*my* true child in *the* faith" (1 Timothy. 1:2). This English translation implies that Timothy came to know Christ through the Apostle Paul. However, there is no basis for "my" in the Greek text. Literally, the phrase reads "a genuine child in the faith."

When Paul went to Derbe and Lystra on his second missionary journey, he heard that Timothy was "well spoken of by the brethren who were in Lystra and Iconium" (Acts 16:2).

After joining Paul at this time, Timothy was with him in many of his travels. Timothy had opportunity to watch Paul's life in times of great victory as well as in the face of bitter opposition.

Timothy was Paul's official representative in Ephesus, as indicated by Paul's words: "As I urged you upon my departure for Macedonia, remain on at Ephesus so that you may instruct certain men not to teach strange doctrines" (1 Tim. 1:3). Timothy needed counsel and encouragement, so Paul used the occasion to write his first letter to him. The epistles, or letters, of 1 and 2 Timothy and Titus are called "Pastoral Epistles" because they give important instruction concerning the pastoral ministry. Actually, the letter to Titus was written between Paul's two letters to Timothy, even though the letters to Timothy are placed together in the English Bible.

The last letter to Timothy, known to us as "2 Timothy," contains the Apostle Paul's last recorded words. Approximately 15 years had elapsed since Timothy had joined Paul on the second missionary journey. Many things had transpired since that time, and now the Apostle Paul was in prison in Rome. This was a different imprisonment than the one mentioned in Acts 28. In the earlier imprisonment, Paul was accused of heresy by the Jews, was allowed to preach freely to those who visited him at his own rented quarters and was looking forward to being released.

However, as he wrote his second letter to Timothy from prison, Paul was being persecuted by the Romans, could be visited only with great difficulty, and was expecting death at any time. During the earlier imprisonment, he wrote the letters commonly referred to as the "Prison Epistles"—Philemon, Colossians, Ephesians and Philippians. During his last imprisonment, he wrote only 2 Timothy.

The prisons of Paul's day were not like those of today. Paul likely wrote his last letter from a damp dungeon, which gave him reason to tell Timothy: "When you come bring the cloak which I left at Troas with Carpus, and the books, especially the parchments" (2 Tim. 4:13) and also to urge Timothy: "Make every effort to come before winter" (v. 21).

Although the normal reaction in such a place would be extreme despondency, there is a note of victory throughout Paul's last letter to Timothy. He was looking forward to being with the Lord Jesus Christ. As Paul charged Timothy concerning the Christian faith, there were no regrets implied by Paul for what he had suffered. He was enthralled with the love and grace of God; this is why he had served Christ without reservation.

Paul wrote his last letter to Timothy from Rome in about A.D. 67. Three years earlier, there had been a great fire in Rome, and many thought that Nero, the emperor, had set the fire. In order to place the blame on others, Nero accused the followers of Christ of having started the fire, and a great persecution broke out against them. Whenever Christians are persecuted, the known Christian leaders are intensely sought. Paul was such a leader, and he was arrested on false charges. He told Timothy: "for which I suffer hardship even to imprisonment as a criminal; but the word of God is not imprisoned" (2 Tim. 2:9).

Paul had been in prison before, but it had been for preaching the gospel. Now he was in prison on a false charge—perhaps the charge of having helped to set the fire in Rome. But even under these adverse circumstances, the Apostle Paul was not feeling sorry for himself. He was concerned about magnifying the Lord Jesus Christ not only in deed but also in attitude.

Realizing that death could come at any time, Paul wrote his last letter to Timothy to encourage the younger man in the Christian faith, regardless of how insurmountable the obstacles might seem.

Chapter 2 – Paul's Greeting

ANY PERSON'S LAST words before death are significant. As stated in Chapter 1, the epistle of 2 Timothy is especially important because it contains the last inspired words written by the Apostle Paul. Because Paul wrote by inspiration of the Holy Spirit, the message of 2 Timothy is profitable to those living in every age. That Paul was expecting death as he wrote gives a special urgency to the message of his last letter to Timothy. Paul began his letter with the words:

Paul, an apostle of Christ Jesus according to the promise of life in Christ Jesus (1:1).

In Paul's time it was customary for the letter writer to introduce himself before addressing the individual to whom he was writing. Thus, Paul placed his own name first.

Paul was also known by the name "Saul." He was referred to as "Saul" in the early chapters of the Book of Acts, but the name "Paul" is used in the last half of Acts and in the epistles. Some interpreters maintain that at the time of his conversion he adopted the Gentile name "Paul" in place of his Hebrew name "Saul." It is more likely, however, that Paul used both names from his early years, as was customary in those days. After his conversion he probably used his Gentile name (Paul) most of the time to more closely identify himself as an apostle to the Gentiles (see Gal. 2:7-8).

Writing to Timothy, Paul described himself as "an apostle of Christ Jesus." The Greek word translated "apostle" is *apostolos*, which means "one sent on a mission," or "a messenger." In a general sense, every believer is sent as an ambassador of Jesus Christ. Earlier, Paul had written: "Therefore, we are ambassadors for Christ, as though God were making an appeal through us; we beg you on behalf of Christ, be reconciled to God" (2 Cor. 5:20). However, Paul was a "sent one" in a special sense, because he had been chosen by Jesus Christ to be an apostle. Paul always marveled at the grace of God in choosing him to be an apostle (1 Cor. 15:8-10).

In this greeting the name "Jesus" is the English transliteration for the Greek name *Iesous*, which, in turn, is from the Hebrew name *Jehoshua*, meaning "Jehovah saves." The significance of the name "Jesus" is seen in what the angel of the Lord told Joseph: "She [Mary] will bear a Son; and you shall call His name Jesus, for He will save His people from their sins" (Matt. 1:21). The name "Christ" is from the Greek word *Christos*, that signified to Israel that Jesus was the anointed Messiah. Of Andrew, the Scriptures say: "He found first his own brother Simon and said to him, 'We have found the Messiah' (which translated means Christ)" (John 1:41).

Paul's apostleship had often been attacked, so even in writing to Timothy, Paul described himself as "an apostle…by the will of God." Many were saying that men had appointed Paul an apostle, but Paul underscored the fact that his call to apostleship was "by the will of God," not by the commandment of men. Certainly, Timothy would not question Paul's apostleship, but Paul's reminder concerning his apostleship by the will of God emphasized the importance of what he was writing to Timothy.

Paul also reminded Timothy that his apostleship was "according to the promise of life in Christ Jesus." Paul was constantly thrilled with the eternal life he had in Christ. Earlier, he had urged Timothy on to godliness by saying that "godliness is profitable for all things, since it holds promise for the present life and *also* for the *life* to come" (1 Tim. 4:8). In writing to Titus, Paul referred to "the hope of eternal life, which God, who cannot lie, promised long ages ago" (Titus 1:2).

In 2 Timothy 1:1 the words "in Christ" are especially significant. These words are used only of those who receive salvation during the Church Age. At the time of salvation, the Holy Spirit baptizes, or places, believers into the Body of Christ (1 Cor. 12:13). The words "in Christ" emphasize the position that all present-day believers have. This phrase or similar ones are frequently used throughout Paul's epistles, especially in the Book of Ephesians. Ephesians 1:3 summarizes the believer's position in Christ: "Blessed be the God and Father of our Lord Jesus Christ, who has blessed us with every spiritual blessing in the heavenly *places* in Christ."

To Timothy, my beloved son: Grace, mercy *and* peace from God the Father and Christ Jesus our Lord (1:2).

Having introduced himself as the writer, Paul then greeted Timothy, to whom his letter was addressed. As mentioned previously, information about Timothy can be found in Acts 16 and the First Epistle of Paul to Timothy.

Paul referred to Timothy as "my beloved son." As in 1 Timothy 1:2, there is no support for the word "my" in the Greek text. Literally, the phrase reads, "a beloved child."

The word "beloved" is one of the strongest words Paul could use to express his love for Timothy, for it is a form of the Greek verb *agapaō*, which emphasizes a love so great that it loves even when there is no response.

The word "son" would be better translated "child." The Greek word involved is *teknon*. Rather than emphasizing adult sonship, *teknon* stresses the birth aspect of sonship. The verb form means "to beget," or "to bring forth"; thus, the noun refers to the one who had been begotten, or brought forth. The noun form of this Greek word is used in John 1:12, where the more accurate translation is "children of God" rather than "sons of God."

In referring to Timothy as a beloved child, Paul emphasized Timothy's spiritual birth and training. Although it is not known conclusively that Paul was the one who led Timothy to the Lord, at least Paul had a significant part in Timothy's spiritual training.

To Timothy, Paul wrote: "Grace, mercy and peace." "Grace" was one of Paul's key words. He never ceased to be amazed at God's salvation by grace through faith, Paul was especially sensitive about his lost condition before salvation and always marveled that God loved him so much. Grace emphasizes unmerited favor that God shows to mankind. Salvation is of grace; it is to be received, not earned (Eph. 2:8-9).

"Mercy" refers to God's consideration of man in his misery of sin. Grace and mercy are related. Because of God's mercy, He extends His grace to mankind. And because of His grace, God is also able to extend mercy to man in his misery of sin. The gift of salvation provides the payment for the penalty of sin and breaks the power of sin. Someday, when the believer goes to be with Christ, he will be delivered from the presence of sin.

"Peace" was also emphasized by the Apostle Paul. He lived in a world that knew little peace. The corrupt Roman government of his time was a hard taskmaster. Christians had special reasons to fear, because Rome saw them as enemies of the government, so it persecuted them and put many of them to death. But Paul knew that, regardless of the circumstances, it is possible for the believer to have peace.

Peace with God is acquired at the time of salvation. Paul said, "Therefore, having been justified by faith, we have peace with God through our Lord Jesus Christ" (Rom. 5:1). But not all who have peace *with* God have the peace *of* God. Paul urged believers: "Be anxious for nothing, but in everything by prayer and supplication with thanksgiving let your requests be known to God. And the peace of God, which surpasses all comprehension, will guard your hearts and your minds in

Christ Jesus" (Phil. 4:6-7).

In Paul's salutation to Timothy, he referred to grace, mercy and peace as being "from God the Father and Christ Jesus our Lord." Grace, mercy and peace originate in the Father and the Son. Paul did not mention the Holy Spirit in this case; however, it is clear elsewhere in the Scriptures that the ministry of the Spirit is to take what originates with the Father and the Son and to apply it to the believer's life. Concerning the Holy Spirit, the Lord Jesus said, "But when He, the Spirit of truth, comes, He will guide you into all the truth; for He will not speak on His own initiative, but whatever He hears, He will speak; and He will disclose to you what is to come. He will glorify Me, for He will take of Mine and will disclose *it* to you" (John 16:13-14).

In his salutation to Timothy, Paul clearly set forth the riches that every believer has in Christ. Now Paul is ready to share with Timothy the burdens that are on his heart.

Chapter 3 - Paul's Fond Memories

AFTER HIS SALUTATION to Timothy (2 Tim. 1:1-2), Paul expressed his gratitude to God. He wrote:

I thank God, whom I serve with a clear conscience the way my forefathers did, as I constantly remember you in my prayers night and day (1:3).

The words "I thank God" literally mean, "I am having gratitude to God." Paul was thankful not only at that moment, but he was constantly having gratitude to God. Being thankful was one of Paul's prominent characteristics. To the Thessalonians he wrote: "in everything give thanks; for this is God's will for you in Christ Jesus" (1 Thess. 5:18). As Paul wrote 2 Timothy he was suffering hardship in a Roman prison, but in spite of this he was constantly giving thanks to God.

Paul said of God, "whom I serve with a clear conscience the way my forefathers did." The word translated "serve" is *latreuō*, which is always used in the Bible to refer to religious service or worship. Paul had been involved in religious service even before he was born again. Paul told the Galatians: "For you have heard of my former manner of life in Judaism, how I used to persecute the church of God beyond measure and tried to destroy it; and I was advancing in Judaism beyond many of my contemporaries among my countrymen, being more extremely zealous for my ancestral traditions" (Gal. 1:13-14). But even though Paul was so religiously zealous, he did not have eternal life until the Lord appeared to him when he was on his way to Damascus (Acts 9).

Paul told Timothy that he served God with a "clear conscience." "Clear" is a translation of a Greek form of *katharos* which means "clean or pure." Paul had a clear conscience even before he was saved because of his religious service. This shows that sincerity, or a clear conscience, is not the test of salvation. After Paul received Christ as Savior he reflected on his past life and said, "But whatever things were gain to me, those things I have counted as loss for the sake of Christ" (Phil. 3:7).

Paul went on to tell Timothy: "as I constantly remember you in my prayers night and day." The words "constantly remember" are translated from the word *adialeiptos*. The same Greek word appears in 1 Thessalonians 5:17: "Pray without ceasing." This does not mean that one is to pray a single, never-ending prayer; rather he is to pray *constantly*. ("Constant" implies uniform or persistent recurrence.) Examples from secular literature in New Testament times use the word in referring to a cough. Such a cough would not be a single, unending cough but rather a series of coughs at brief intervals. As one coughs constantly, so the believer ought to pray constantly. Throughout the night and day in the Roman prison, Paul remembered Timothy and prayed constantly for him.

Longing to see you, even as I recall your tears, so that I may be filled with joy (1:4).

This verse reveals that the seasoned apostle longed for his disciple. Paul and Timothy had been together through many circumstances, and now that he was in prison, Paul longed to see Timothy once more. This reveals the desire for fellowship that Paul had. No matter how mature a Christian becomes, it is never good for him to be away from the fellowship of other believers for a prolonged time. This is why Hebrews 10:25 says, "not forsaking our own assembling together, as is the habit of some, but encouraging *one another*; and all the more as you see the day drawing near."

Paul told Timothy that he greatly longed to see him, "even as I recall your tears." Timothy had apparently expressed great sorrow when Paul had a longing to see him again. Paul's purpose in wanting to see Timothy was expressed in these words: "That I may filled with joy." Again, these words showed the appreciation Paul had for fellowship with other believers; it supplied a joy that could not be provided in any other way.

For I am mindful of the sincere faith within you, which first dwelt in your grandmother Lois and your mother Eunice, and I am sure that *it* is in you as well (1:5).

Notice what Paul remembered about Timothy—his "sincere faith." The memory of Timothy's faith encouraged Paul while he was in prison and gave him a great longing to see him. The word translated "sincere" literally means "unhypocritical." Timothy had a consistent faith. He did not put on an act by doing certain things to impress others.

Paul told Timothy that the same kind of faith "first dwelt in your grandmother Lois and your mother Eunice." This is the only time that Timothy's mother and grandmother are referred to by name. Although her name is not given, Timothy's mother is referred to in Acts 16:1: "Paul came also to Derbe and to Lystra. And a disciple was there, named Timothy, the son of a Jewish woman who was a believer, but his father was a Greek."

It seems significant that the grandmother, mother and son all had an unhypocritical faith. The example of the parent had its effect on the child. Here we see the spiritual principle: "Train up a child in the way he should go, even when he is old he will not depart from it" (Prov. 22:6). The example of the parent had been reproduced in the child.

Referring to the faith that was in his grandmother and mother, Paul told Timothy: "and I am sure that *it* is in you as well." In making this statement, Paul used a Greek tense which indicated that he had been persuaded in the past and was still persuaded that Timothy also possessed this same kind of faith. The experiences that Paul and Timothy had shared together proved to Paul beyond doubt that Timothy's faith was an unhypocritical one. There was nothing phony about Timothy. When he remembered the quality of Timothy's faith, the Apostle Paul greatly longed to see him again.

Chapter 4 – Rekindling God's Gift

AFTER EXPRESSING HIS longing to see Timothy and his remembrance of Timothy's unhypocritical faith, Paul went on to say,

For this reason I remind you to kindle afresh the gift of God which is in you through the laying of hands (1:6).

Paul reminded Timothy to "kindle afresh the gift of God." The veteran missionary and apostle believed it was necessary to remind Timothy of this need. In the activities of life, believers sometimes fail to think about certain responsibilities as they should unless they are reminded to do so. Apparently Paul felt it a part of his spiritual responsibility to Timothy to remind him of certain duties.

The words "kindle afresh" are a translation of *anazōpureō* which means to "keep in full flame," and the tense of this verb emphasizes continuous action. Paul wanted Timothy to continually stir the coals to keep the fire burning brightly in his life.

Kindling the fire continually had to do with the "gift of God." In Paul's previous letter he told Timothy, "Do not neglect the spiritual gift within you, which was bestowed on you through prophetic utterance with the laying on of hands by the presbytery" (1 Tim. 4:14). In this second epistle Paul referred to the gift "which is in you through the laying of hands." Perhaps Paul refers to the same incident in these two verses. The specific gift was not named, but it seems to have been a ministerial gift of some kind.

"The laying of hands" reveals the background of the present practice of most ordination services. Recognizing that God has called a particular person to the ministry, those participating in the service place their hands on the candidate; thus, they identify themselves with the candidate and acknowledge that they believe God has called him to the ministry. It is possible, however, that in this verse the phrase "through the laying of hands" refers to a special gift which was bestowed by an apostle.

Having reminded Timothy to keep his gift in full flame, Paul explained,

For God has not given us a spirit of timidity, but of power and love and discipline (1:7).

The word "spirit" in this verse does not refer to the Holy Spirit but to an inner quality of life. One of the things God does not give the believer is the spirit of fear. The word Paul used for timidity was *deilia* which means "cowardice." Paul reminded Timothy that the spirit of cowardice did not originate with God. Instead, what originated with God was power. Here Paul used the word *dunamis*, which stresses the power of ability, rather than *exousia* which stresses the power of authority.

As Timothy served Jesus Christ, he would be particularly sensitive to his need for ability. Paul reminded Timothy that God gives this ability. The same word for power is used in Acts 1:8, which records what the Lord told His disciples: "But you will receive power [*dunamis*] when the Holy Spirit has come upon you; and you shall be My witnesses both in Jerusalem, and in all Judea and Samaria, and even to the remotest part or the earth."

Paul also reminded Timothy that love comes from God. Paul did not refer to a spirit of humanitarianism nor to a kind of love which loves only when there is a response. Paul used the word agapē, which refers to the highest level of love. It is the kind of love that loves even when there is no response. This kind of love always seeks the highest good of the other person, even though that person may despise the one who loves him.

The same word for love was used by the Lord when He said, "Love your enemies" (Matt. 5:44). The kind of love that Paul and the Lord referred to cannot be achieved by human determination; it originates with God, and only those who know Jesus Christ as Savior have the capacity to love in this way. This kind of love is the fruit of the Spirit, which should be seen in every believer's life.

Paul reminded Timothy that in addition to power and love, "discipline" originates with God. Paul was referring to the kind of sound mind that results in self-control. Paul saw nothing spiritual about an undisciplined life, because this is the opposite of what the believer ought to be. The discipline of Paul's life is expressed in such passages as 1 Corinthians 9:24-27 and Philippians 3:10-14, where he viewed the Christian life as a race in which the runner must exercise self-control as he runs toward the finish line.

Having reminded Timothy of these important truths, Paul exhorted him:

Therefore do not be ashamed of the testimony of our Lord or of me His prisoner, but join with *me* in suffering for the gospel according to the power of God (1:8).

In the light of the fact that God has not given the believer a spirit of cowardice but of power, love and discipline, there is no legitimate reason for the believer to be ashamed of the Lord. Although some might interpret this verse as meaning that Timothy was ashamed, it seems to be more of an encouragement by Paul that Timothy should never be ashamed.

Paul urged Timothy not to be ashamed about two matters: "the testimony of our Lord" and "of me His prisoner." Paul was concerned that Timothy not be ashamed of the Lord and that he not be ashamed of him, his teacher.

Paul's imprisonment may have caused some believers embarrassment and shame because they had misunderstood why Paul was in prison. In Paul's statement, however, we catch a glimpse of his victorious attitude. Paul did not consider himself a prisoner of the Roman government; he considered himself a prisoner of the Lord. As far as Paul was concerned, God was still on the throne, so he did not have a defeated attitude because of his circumstances.

Paul urged Timothy, "Join with *me* in suffering for the gospel." The words "join with me in suffering" are a translation of the single Greek word *sugkakopatheō*, which means "to bear evil treatment along with." Paul wanted Timothy to be willing to suffer evil treatment along with him for the sake of the gospel. Even this was to be "according to the power of God."

Although Paul might have complained and had a defeatist attitude because of his circumstances, we see him here at the end of his life having no regrets for what he had suffered for the gospel. He even encouraged others to suffer along with him. If Paul had been able to live his life over, he would have not taken any shortcuts or made any compromises to avoid suffering for the gospel's sake. Because he appreciated the grace of God and realized that others needed to hear the gospel, Paul was willing to suffer whatever was necessary to proclaim that gospel to others.

Chapter 5 - Saved to Serve

PAUL URGED TIMOTHY: "Join with me in suffering for the gospel according to the power of God" (2 Tim. 1:8). Having mentioned God, Paul tells about Him in the following verse:

Who has saved us and called us with a holy calling, not according to our works, but according to His own purpose and grace which was granted us in Christ Jesus from all eternity (1:9).

The words "saved" and "called" are Greek aorist participles. Therefore, they can literally be translated "having saved" and "having called." Paul was referring to past acts of God—God was not then saving and calling Paul and Timothy. The word "saved" does not always have a spiritual meaning in Greek, just as it does not always have a spiritual meaning in English. The context must tell what one is being saved from. Here it does have the spiritual meaning, for Paul is talking about salvation from condemnation.

John 3:17 uses the word "saved" in a spiritual sense: "For God did not send the Son into the world to judge the world, but that the world might be saved through Him." It is apparent from the first phrase of the following verse that this word refers to being saved from condemnation: "He who believers in Him is not judged."

Paul also reminded Timothy that they had been "called" by

God. Paul frequently marveled that God chose him as an object of grace. He told the Ephesians, "Blessed *be* the God and Father of our Lord Jesus Christ, who has blessed us with every spiritual blessing in the heavenly *places* in Christ, just as He chose us in Him before the foundation of the world, that we would be holy and blameless before Him in love" (1:3-4). Paul knew that each believer's salvation had been planned by the Father before the world came into existence. This caused him to marvel even more at the grace of God.

Paul explained to Timothy that God had called them "with a holy calling." Both the form of the word in Greek and the context indicate that the word "with" is better translated "to." Any calling from God would be holy, but Paul seemed to be emphasizing that God had called him and Timothy—and all believers—*to* that holy calling. This parallels what Paul said in Ephesians 1:4: "He chose us in Him before the foundation of the world, that we would be holy and blameless before Him." Paul had been endeavoring to encourage Timothy to "join with [him] in suffering for the gospel according to the power of God" (v. 8); therefore, he reminded Timothy that God had saved and called him to a holy calling.

Paul further explained that God's saving and calling work was "according to His own purpose and grace." This statement reveals that an individual cannot, by his own words, merit a position before God. To the Ephesians, Paul expressed this truth in these words: "For by grace you have been saved through faith; and that not of yourselves, *it is* the gift of God; not as a result of works, so that no one may boast" (2:8-9). In contrast, an individual's salvation is "according to His own purpose and grace" (2 Tim. 1:9). God has done it all for every individual; all the individual needs to do is receive God's unmerited favor and believe in Jesus as Savior.

Concerning God's grace, or unmerited favor, Paul told Timothy that it "was granted us in Christ Jesus from all eternity." This was Paul's way of saying that God's grace to man was already conceived in the mind of God in a time so remote that it is inconceivable to the imagination of any person. The following verse reveals how God displayed His grace:

But now has been revealed by the appearing of our Savior Christ Jesus, who abolished death and brought life and immortality to light through the gospel (1:10).

Although God's grace was granted to the believer from eternity past, it was especially revealed through the appearing of Jesus Christ.

The word translated "appearing" is *epiphaneia*, which was commonly used in the secular Greek of Paul's day. The Greeks frequently used this word in referring to a glorious manifestation of one of their gods. Paul used the word to refer to the appearance of the true God. The time of this appearance to which Paul referred was the first coming of the Lord Jesus Christ. The Son of God "became flesh, and dwelt among us" (John 1:14). The Lord Jesus Christ became human, so He could die on the cross and pay the penalty for sin. This is why Paul referred to Him as "our Savior Christ Jesus" (2 Tim. 1:10). God's purpose and grace was especially revealed when Jesus Christ appeared in human form because He had come to be the Savior of the world.

Having mentioned Jesus Christ, Paul proceeded to tell what He had done: "Who abolished death and brought life and immorality to light through the gospel." This statement reveals both the destructive and the constructive work of Christ—He abolished death and brought life and immorality to light.

The word translated "abolished" is *katargeō* which means "to render idle, inactive, inoperative." Death was not completely done away with at the first coming of Jesus Christ, but because of the salvation He provided, death no longer has the power it once had. Those placing their trust in Christ can look beyond death; therefore, they do not need to live their lives in fear or death. This is why Paul was able to write: "O death, where is your victory? O death, where is your sting?"

(1 Cor. 15:55).

Physical death will not be eliminated until God has concluded His program for this world. Revelation 21:4 refers to that future time when "He will wipe away every tear from their eyes; and there will no longer be *any* death; there will no longer be *any* mourning, or crying, or pain; the first things have passed away." But how wonderful it is that even now believers can look beyond the grave to the time when they will be with Christ because of what He accomplished by coming to earth to pay the penalty for sin.

In His first coming, Christ also "brought life and immortality to light through the gospel." The hope of eternal life and immortality was present before Christ's first coming, but it was by His coming that He brought them "to light"—He focused special attention on them. His own resurrection, which Paul frequently refers to as a crucial part of the gospel, especially focused attention on life and immortality. In fact, Christ's resurrection provides the assurance to believers that they also will be resurrected (1 Cor. 15:12-19).

Paul said that Christ focused attention on life and immortality, or incorruption, "through the gospel." As indicated by 1 Corinthians 15:1-4, the gospel message is the death, burial and resurrection of Jesus Christ. As the gospel is proclaimed today it continues to focus attention on life and immortality.

The word translated "gospel" means "good news." It is the good news that by the death, burial and resurrection of Jesus Christ salvation has been provided for all, and that anyone can have forgiveness of sin and eternal life by receiving Him as Savior. Having referred to the gospel, Paul went on to explain his relationship to it.

For which I was appointed a preacher and an apostle and a teacher (1:11).

Paul had a threefold relationship to the gospel: God had appointed him to be a teacher, an apostle and a teacher.

The word for "preacher" is *kērux*, which means "a herald" or a messenger." The word was commonly used in Paul's time to refer to one who made a public announcement as ordered by another. It was used of the imperial herald, who made a public proclamation of the emperor's message. Paul had been appointed by God to be a herald of the death, burial and resurrection of Jesus Christ.

Paul was also appointed to be "an apostle." An apostle was one sent forth with orders. This word emphasized Paul's authority concerning the message. An apostle was also one who had been with Jesus. Although Paul was not counted as one of the 12 apostles, Jesus appeared to him on his way to Damascus. Referring to this time, Paul later wrote, "And last of all, as to one untimely born, He appeared to me also. For I am the least of the apostles, and not fit to be called an apostle, because I persecuted the church of God" (1 Cor. 15:8-9).

Paul was also a "teacher" of the gospel. This word reveals the method he used in imparting the message of others. He presented the gospel in an orderly manner and explained its significance to others.

Chapter 6 –
Confidence in God's
Ability

**For this reason I also suffer these things, but I am not
ashamed; for I know whom I have believed and I am
convinced that He is able to guard what I have entrusted
to Him until that day. (1:12).**

"FOR THIS REASON" continues the thought of Paul's
relationship to the gospel. The result of his relationship to it is
explained in his words "I also suffer these things." He did not
enumerate the things he was suffering, apparently because
they were well known to Timothy. It is evident from his
words "Therefore do not be ashamed of the testimony about
our Lord or of me His prisoner, but join with *me* in suffering
for the gospel according to the power of God" (v. 8). In verse
12, Paul emphasized to Timothy that he was not ashamed
because of his relationship to the gospel.

Paul explained why he was not ashamed: "For I know
whom I have believed and I am convinced that He is able to
guard what I have entrusted to Him until that day." Paul's
trust was centered in a person—the Lord Jesus Christ.
Whereas unbelievers usually think that being associated with
Jesus Christ brings shame, it was Paul's relationship with
Jesus Christ that kept him from being ashamed.

Paul said, "I know whom I have believed and I am

convinced." The Greek words translated "believed" and "convinced" are in the past tense, which indicates an act which has been completed in the past with a continuing effect. Paul had believed in Christ in the past, and the effect had continued. He had been persuaded of certain things in the past and still remained persuaded of them.

Paul was persuaded that the One whom he had believed was, as he wrote, "able to guard what I have entrusted to Him until that day." Greek expositors differ on what they think is the meaning of the phrase. From the original language, it is possible to interpret it two ways: (1) Paul had committed the safekeeping of his soul to God and was confident that God would guard it until a future day, or (2) God had committed the gospel message to Paul, and God would safeguard the message.

When two such legitimate interpretations are possible, one must carefully examine the context to see which is preferred. From the context, it is evident that the emphasis was on Paul's service in proclaiming the gospel, not on his salvation as such. The word translated "entrusted" is *parathēkē*, which actually means "deposited." The same thought was stated later when Paul told Timothy, "Guard, through the Holy Spirit who dwells in us, the treasure which has been entrusted [*parathēkē*] to you" (v. 14).

The last words of verse 12, "until that day," refer to the time when Paul will stand before the Lord Jesus Christ to be rewarded for the way he served Christ. Paul spoke of the time in 2 Corinthians 5:10: "For we must all appear before the judgment seat of Christ, so that each one may be recompensed for his deeds in the body, according to what he has done, whether good or bad."

Regardless of what the believer must suffer in this life, his confidence need not be shaken, because God will always be faithful on his behalf. He will someday be rewarded if he has served Christ well.

Having said that he was not ashamed, Paul appealed to Timothy:

Retain the standard of sound words which you have heard from me, in the faith and love which are in Christ Jesus (1:13).

The word "retain" is a translation of *echō* meaning "to have." This Greek word stresses possession and indicates that Paul was concerned that Timothy would tightly hold to "the standard of sound words."

The word translated "standard" means "a sketch," or "outline." A form of this same Greek word was used to describe an impression left by a seal, and the imprint, or effect left by the blow. As such it came to mean "pattern" or "model." As an artist works from a sketch, Timothy was to align his preaching and teaching to that pattern, or example, that Paul had set for him. That the pattern had been set by Paul is indicated by the words: "which you have heard from me."

The word translated "sound" means "healthy." It was commonly used in New Testament times to refer not only to health but also to something that was wholesome, fit or wise. Paul considered it urgent that Timothy keep the pattern of teaching that Paul had established for him.

Paul qualified how Timothy was to adhere to this pattern of sound words: "In the faith and love which are in Christ Jesus." Timothy was to daily exercise his faith in the provisions he had in Christ, and his life was to be characterized by love. As he defended the gospel, Timothy was to give evidence of the fruit of the Spirit—love. Untold damage has been caused by Christians who have tenaciously defended the gospel but who have not shown love while doing so. Along with holding fast the form of sound words, Paul appealed to Timothy:

Guard, through the Holy Spirit who dwells in us, the treasure which has been entrusted to you (1:14).

Paul further emphasized Timothy's relation to the gospel

by exhorting him to keep, or guard, "the treasure which has been entrusted to you." It is the healthy teaching (sound words) of verse 13 that is seen as committed, or deposited, with Timothy in verse 14. Paul not only wanted Timothy to cling to the pattern that had been set for him but also to defend, or guard, what had been deposited to him. In verse 12 Paul trusted God to preserve the message that had been deposited with him; now Paul also wanted Timothy to trust God to preserve that message. Although Paul realized that God must work to preserve the gospel, he realized that individual believers have personal responsibility to guard it.

Just as Paul had previously qualified how Timothy was to retain the pattern of healthy words ("in the faith and love which are in Christ Jesus"), he also qualified how Timothy was to guard the message: "through the Holy Spirit who dwells in us."

Although every ability he had would be used in the process, Timothy was not to depend on himself but on the Holy Spirit. Timothy was to apply the truth of Proverbs 3:5: "Trust in the Lord with all your heart and do not lean on your own understanding."

In referring to the Holy Spirit, Paul said, "who dwells in us." The ministry of the Holy Spirit is to live in the believer and to empower him to accomplish God's will. As Timothy relied on the indwelling Holy Spirit to give him wisdom and power, he would be effective in defending and proclaiming the gospel which had been committed to him.

Chapter 7 – Deserters and Devoted Friends

HAVING ENCOURAGED TIMOTHY to guard that which the Holy Spirit had entrusted to him, Paul went on to tell how Christians had reacted to his imprisonment.

You are aware of the fact that all who are in Asia turned away from me, among whom are Phygelus and Hermogenes (1:15).

By "Asia" Paul referred to that Roman province in the western part of what is now Turkey. Paul had taken the gospel to these people on his missionary journeys and many had received Christ as Savior. Now that Paul was in prison, however, he said that "all who are in Asia turned away from me."

It is possible that Paul meant that these people had gone off into heresy. This is not necessarily implied; however, by his use of the word *apostrephō*, which means "turn away" or "turn back." The verse does not say that they had turned away from Jesus Christ; rather they had turned away from Paul. Apparently they were ashamed of Paul or were at least afraid to be associated with him while he was a prisoner. Imagine the sorrow it must have caused Paul to think that those he had led to Christ were ashamed of being associated with him. And think of his frustration because he was not free to go to these people to explain and help them understand.

Of those who had turned away from him, Paul singled out

two by name—Phygelus and Hermogenes. Because nothing else is said of these two men, it is reasonable to assume that Timothy knew them so there was no reason for Paul to further explain. In contrast to those who were ashamed of him, Paul said:

The Lord grant mercy to the house of Onesiphorus, for he often refreshed me and was not ashamed of my chains (1:16).

The word translated "house" is *oikos* and was used in referring either to a building (house) or to the people that inhabited a building (household, family). In verse 16 Paul was apparently concerned about the family of Onesiphorus and was asking the Lord to show mercy to them because of what Onesiphorus had done for him. Apparently this family lived in Ephesus, because Timothy was ministering there at that time, and at the end of Paul's letter he sent greetings to the family through Timothy (4:19).

Paul explained what Onesiphorus had done for him: "For he often refreshed me and was not ashamed of my chains." The word *anapsuchō* translated "refreshed" means "to cool again, to cool off." It referred to recovering from the effects of heat and also to being revived by fresh air. From this word we see how important Christian fellowship was to Paul. It was like a breath of fresh air; it left him refreshed.

Paul was especially impressed that Onesiphorus was not ashamed of his chains. That is, Onesiphorus did not avoid visiting Paul in prison because of what might happen to him personally as a result of his friendship with a Christian prisoner. Apparently this risk kept other believers from associating with Paul in prison. Paul's reference to "my chains" indicates that he was chained to a guard. Because of this, Paul's activity was very limited, and nothing could be discussed with a fellow believer without being overheard. In spite of this, Paul said concerning Onesiphorus:

But when he was in Rome, he eagerly searched for me and found me (1:17).

These words indicate that it was not an easy task for someone to find Paul. However, Onesiphorus did not give up—he sought "eagerly." This word is a translation of *spoudaiōs* which was used in New Testament times to refer not just to diligence but to "utmost diligence." You can almost see Onesiphorus going from door to door in his search for Paul. Onesiphorus's persistent search showed his courage—he wanted to fellowship with Paul regardless of the cost.

Paul must have been glad to report that Onesiphorus "found me." It had been fellowship with Onesiphorus that refreshed Paul in the Roman prison. Thus Paul said:

The Lord grant to him to find mercy from the Lord on that day—and you know very well what services he rendered at Ephesus (1:18).

Although it is not known what it cost Onesiphorus to fellowship with the Apostle Paul, some think this verse and verse 16 indicate that it had cost Onesiphorus his life. In verse 16, Paul was asking the Lord to give mercy to the family of Onesiphorus, but he did not ask the same for Onesiphorus. So it is possible that Onesiphorus was no longer living. In verse 18 Paul asked the Lord to grant mercy "on that day"—which probably refers to the day of judgment for believers. Again, a possible implication is that Onesiphorus was no longer living at the time Paul wrote these words.

However, these verses need not be interpreted to mean Onesiphorus was now dead. Paul may have been especially concerned about the family of Onesiphorus, and the words of verse 16 would be a normal way to express this concern. Onesiphorus may have been living at the time Paul wrote verse 18, and the verse would have been Paul's way of expressing his concern that God richly reward Onesiphorus in the day of the believers' judgment because of what he had done for Paul in Rome. There is not enough information available in these verses to conclusively say whether or not Onesiphorus was living at the time of Paul's writing.

Paul told Timothy: "You know very well what services he rendered at Ephesus." The word translated "services" is *diakoneō*. The word "deacon" is derived from the noun form (*diakonos*) of this word. The word meant "to serve, to minister." Onesiphorus had not only met Paul's needs of spiritual fellowship in prison, but earlier he had also ministered to Paul's needs in Ephesus. There was a strong spiritual bond between Paul and Onesiphorus—a bond so strong that it caused Onesiphorus to risk his life to fellowship with Paul in Rome.

Of the things that Onesiphorus had ministered to Paul in Ephesus, Paul told Timothy "You know very well." The words "very well" are translated from *belitōn*, which means "better." Because Timothy was ministering in Ephesus, he knew better than Paul how Onesiphorus had served him in Ephesus.

The keynote of 2 Timothy 1 is that of not being ashamed. Paul told Timothy "Do not be ashamed" (v. 8). Of himself, Paul said, "I am not ashamed" (v. 12). Paul mentioned those in "Asia" who were ashamed (v. 15) and told of Onesiphorus who "was not ashamed" (v. 16). This chapter serves as a vivid reminder to every Christian that there is pressure from the world, the flesh, and the Devil to be ashamed of Jesus Christ and other believers. But this chapter is also a reminder that "God has not given us a spirit of timidity [cowardice], but of power and love and discipline" (v. 7).

Chapter 8 - The Motivation of Grace

You therefore, my son, be strong in the grace that is in Christ Jesus (2:1).

BY USING THE word "therefore," Paul referred to what had been previously stated. No doubt this involved both his instructions to Timothy in chapter 1 as well as the record of the sad defection of some. Because of both of these matters it was imperative that Timothy heed Paul's exhortation if he was to excel in pleasing God.

In 2:1 Paul referred to Timothy as his "son," as he did in 1:2. In both cases the word also used is *teknon*, which means "child," but it was also used of adults as an endearing term of affection. Its use emphasizes how fond Paul was of Timothy.

Paul told Timothy to "be strong." The word Paul used means "to strengthen." It also implies the idea of power. Paul used the word with the Greek present tense that emphasizes continuous action; thus, he was telling Timothy: "Keep on being empowered" or "Keep on being strengthened."

Paul was not referring to physical strength but to inner spiritual strength. This fact is seen by his words "in the grace that is in Christ Jesus." Paul was telling Timothy of the true source of motivation in the Christian life. It was as if Paul was looking ahead to Timothy's future ministry and was giving him what he needed to make that ministry effective for God. Paul had already told him, "Do not be ashamed of the testimony of our Lord or of *me* his prisoner, but join with me in suffering for the gospel according to the power of God" 1:8). If Timothy heeded Paul's words in 2:1, then he would not be ashamed of the Lord's testimony, and he would be able to suffer for the gospel's sake.

When he specified the true source of motivation, Paul did not appeal to needs, to what others were doing, or to what the Lord commanded; he appealed to grace. One who lives on the basis of needs alone eventually reaches the point where he becomes overwhelmed and discouraged because he realizes he can never adequately meet all the needs. The one who compares himself with his peers, no matter how dedicated they may be, eventually realizes that not every person is capable of doing the same thing, so he tends to slacken in his efforts. The one who serves only because the Lord has specifically commanded him to serve and witness will eventually be characterized by slavish obedience rather than joyful serving. But the one who considers the grace of God as his motivation will constantly be spiritually strengthened, regardless of the obstacles, and will have inexpressible joy in serving the Lord.

Paul knew that if Timothy would focus his attention on the grace of God, he would have a motivation that would never quit. The focal point of this grace is "In Christ Jesus." By itself, God's grace is abstract and difficult to define, but it was demonstrated in what Jesus Christ did for mankind. Even though no one deserved it, He died on the cross to pay the penalty for everyone's sin so that any person could have forgiveness of sin and everlasting life by receiving Him as Savior. The more we think on this fact, the more we will be motivated to take the gospel to others and to visibly demonstrate His love.

Having touched on motivation, Paul then instructed Timothy concerning what he should do:

The things which you have heard from me in the presence of many witnesses, entrust these to faithful men who will

be able to teach others also (2:2).

This verse reveals the multiplication principle that should be seen more in Bible teaching and evangelism. What a person has heard he is to pass on to others, who in turn will pass it on to still others. Sometimes this verse is used to emphasize person-to-person teaching rather than group teaching. Although person-to-person evangelism and teaching is an excellent method, this verse seems to be talking more about a group situation than an individual one. This is seen from the fact that Timothy was to pass on these things he had heard from Paul "in the presence of many witnesses." Certainly Timothy had received the individual instruction from Paul many times, but there were also many times when Timothy heard Paul speak to groups. Many witnesses had heard what Paul had said, and Paul was now telling Timothy to be faithful in passing on this teaching to others.

Notice that Timothy's responsibility was not to pass on new truth but to teach what he had heard from Paul. Paul said, "Entrust these to faithful men who will be able to teach others also." The word translated "entrust" is the same basic word translated "entrusted" in 1:14: "Guard, through the Holy Spirit who dwells in us, the treasure which has been entrusted to you." The word conveys the idea of "deposit." God had deposited a responsibility with Timothy, and Paul had deposited truths in Timothy that Timothy was able to deposit in others.

Paul did not obligate Timothy to spend his life committing these things to just anyone. Rather, he was to commit them to "faithful men." The word translated "men" is *anthrōpos* that includes both men and women. Timothy was to invest his life in those who meant business for the Lord. The believer must be patient with those who do not realize they have a need and be available to help when they do not realize it. The effective believer; however, does not spend significant amounts of time attempting to help those who do not want to be helped. Of course, we are to be faithful in proclaiming the gospel to everyone; but if the world is to be reached with the gospel, it must be done by working through faithful people.

Paul even qualified what faithful men Timothy was to pass these things on to—those "who will be able to teach others also." It was not enough that they be trustworthy; they had to be committed to teaching this information to others. The word translated "able" is *hikanos*, which means "ready" as well as "able" in the sense of "capable." At least two things are involved in order to have capable people who can pass on spiritual truths—a desire on their part, and training by others who are capable. The task of the Church today is to work with those who are serious about the Lord's work and to train them to be effective witnesses in Christ and effective teachers of God's Word.

Chapter 9 – "A Good Soldier of Jesus Christ"

Suffer hardship with *me*, as a good soldier of Christ Jesus (2:3).

IN ENCOURAGING TIMOTHY in his Christian life, Paul told him to "suffer hardship." These words are a translation of a single Greek word (*sugkakopatheō*) which Timothy had seen before in Paul's letter (1:8). Concerning the gospel, Paul had told Timothy to "join with *me* in suffering," which is a translation of the same Greek word. It means "to bear evil treatment along with" or "take one's share of ill treatment." Paul was encouraging Timothy in 1:8 and 2:3 to be willing to suffer ill treatment as he took the gospel to others. Realizing the grace of God and man's need for the gospel, Paul implied that Timothy should suffer anything necessary to take the message of salvation to others.

Paul urged Timothy to suffer ill treatment "as a good soldier." Paul frequently drew an analogy between the believer and a soldier. Paul viewed the believer as engaged in warfare for Christ even as a Roman soldier (*stratiōtēs*) was involved in warfare for the emperor. Paul told the Corinthians "For though we walk in the flesh, we do not war according to the flesh (2 Cor. 10:3). He instructed the Ephesians (and all believers) to put on the whole armor of God because of the spiritual warfare in which each believer is engaged (Eph. 6:11-17).

In his first letter to Timothy, Paul said, "This command I entrust to you, Timothy, *my son*, in accordance with the prophecies previously made concerning you, that by them you fight the good fight" (1:18). From these statements we can see that Paul considered every Christian to be a good soldier, but he was especially concerned that Timothy be a "good soldier" (2 Tim. 2:3).

In continuing his comparison of the Christian to a soldier, Paul said,

No soldier in active service entangles himself in the affairs of everyday life, so that he may please the one who enlisted him as a soldier (2:4).

The Greek verb for "soldier," is *strateuōmai* and means "serving in the army." Paul was saying that no soldier on active duty should become entangled in the affairs of this life.

Some have used this verse to indicate that a Christian should not own property or be involved in business because such things entangle him in this life. The word translated "entangles" is *emplekō*, which means "to weave in" or "to entwine." Paul does not seem to be saying that a Christian should not be involved at all in the affairs of this life, but that he should not become enmeshed in the affairs of this life to the extent that it is impossible for him to free himself to serve Jesus Christ. Perhaps this was Paul's way of saying that no one should be "married to his business." A believer's business, or occupation, should be used to serve the Lord; it should not hinder one from serving the Lord.

In referring to the "affairs" of everyday life, Paul used the word *pragmateia*, which means "business" or "occupation." The word was used particularly of occupations that had to do with the civil life in contrast to the soldier's life. The reason that a Christian soldier is not to be enmeshed by the things of this life is evident from Paul's statement "that he may please the one who enlisted him as a soldier." Again, the word "enlisted" is a military term. Christ has enlisted believers as soldiers, and He, not the things of this life, is to have first place in their lives. It should be the primary concern of every believer to please Jesus Christ in every area of his life.

The terminology of Romans 6:13 is also the terminology of warfare. Paul told believers: "and do not go on presenting the members of your body to sin as instruments of unrighteousness; but present yourselves to God as those alive from the dead, and your members as instruments of righteousness to God." We please Jesus Christ as we present ourselves to Him to carry out His will in every area of life.

Two additional characteristics of a good soldier need to be mentioned. First, he does not live to please himself but to carry out the will of his commanding officer. The Christian's commanding officer is none other than Jesus Christ. The believer is to present himself to Jesus Christ to carry out His will. Christ does not override the will of the believer but desires that the believer exercise his will in executing the will of Christ.

Second, a good soldier is not surprised by adverse circumstances. Rather, the good soldier realizes that the absence of open conflict may indicate that the enemy is setting a trap for him. So also, the Christian soldier should realize that when life seems to be going well, he needs to be cautious about temptation that may come through the world, the flesh or the Devil. Paul told believers: "Therefore let him who thinks he stands take heed that he does not fall" (1 Cor. 10:12).

Chapter 10 – The Athlete and the Farmer

Also if anyone competes as an athlete, he does not win the prize unless he competes according to the rules (2:5).

AS PAUL ENCOURAGED Timothy in the Christian life, he drew his attention to three parallels: a soldier, an athlete and a farmer. Having told Timothy to live the Christian life as a good soldier (vv. 3-4), Paul also told Timothy he should live the Christian life as a good athlete.

Paul's New Testament writings reveal that he was well acquainted with the Greek games of his day. A person striving for the "masteries" was an athlete endeavoring to excel in his sport. However, Paul reminded Timothy that such an athlete "does not win the prize unless he competes according to the rules." The athlete who won the contest was "crowned" with a wreath or garland of flowers. Such a wreath would soon fade and lose its beauty. Paul referred to this when he told the Corinthians: "Everyone who competes in the games exercises self-control in all things. They then do *it* to receive a perishable wreath, but we an imperishable" (1 Cor. 9:25). If the athletes of this world strive so hard to obtain temporal awards, we Christians should be far more zealous in seeking to obtain eternal rewards.

Paul reminded Timothy that athletes who wish to be crowned must compete "according to the rules" (2 Tim. 2:5).

The rules for the Greek games applied not only to the contest itself, but also to preliminary training. Before the actual games, athletes subjected themselves to ten months of rigorous training and diet. They had to keep the rules in their training program, and they had to keep them while participating in the contest if they were to win the prize.

In telling Timothy of the athlete, Paul seemed to be reminding him—and all believers—that those who excel in pleasing Christ and are crowned are those who are disciplined in their way of life. The athlete must give up many good things as he trains rigorously for his sport. The Christian must also set priorities and follow them closely if he is to live a well-ordered life that pleases the Lord if he is to accomplish what the Lord wants him to do. As to the rules involved, one of the greatest "rules" of the Christian life is that "the righteous man shall live by faith" (Rom. 1:17). The believer who pleases the Lord is the one whose confidence is in the Lord, not in himself.

Paul then drew another parallel to the Christian life:

The hard-working farmer ought to be the first to receive his share of the crops (2:6).

The word translated "farmer" is *georgos* and means "a tiller of the soil." Paul was reminding Timothy that if he was to excel in the Christian life he must be like a good farmer. The word Paul used for labor implies hard, wearisome toil. The Christian who desires to excel for the Lord cannot be lazy; he must be willing to put forth effort in carrying out the Lord's will for his life.

Concerning the farmer, Paul said that he "ought to be the first to receive his share of the crops." Any farmer who is successful must share in the benefits of his crops if he is to continue planting and harvesting crops in future seasons. So also, the Christian must share the benefits of the gospel in his own life if he is to be effective in ministering to the spiritual needs of others. If the Word of God has not spiritually enriched the believer's life, it will only seem like so much information as he shares the truths of God's Word with others. The word translated "receive" is in the Greek present tense that emphasizes continuous action. The believer must be continually receiving spiritual food from God's Word if he is to be effective in sowing the Word in the lives of others.

In the three parallels that Paul drew to the Christian life, the soldier (vv. 3-4) emphasizes the hardships the believer can expect as he seeks to please the Lord. The athlete (v. 5) illustrates that many good things must be set aside and only the best chosen if the Christian is to be rewarded by the Lord. The farmer (v. 6) emphasizes that the believer must personally and continuously share in the blessings of the Word of God if he is to be effective in reaping a spiritual harvest in the lives of others. Paul then told Timothy:

Consider what I say, for the Lord will give you understanding in everything (2:7).

Paul wanted Timothy to carefully think about these three parallels to the Christian life. The word translated "consider" is *noeō*, which means "to perceive with the mind, to understand." As Timothy thought on these things, he had the promise that the Lord would give him understanding.

The last part of this verse indicates a prayer by Paul: "for the Lord will give you understanding in everything." As Timothy thought on these matters, the Lord would give him the understanding necessary to know how he was to live the Christian life. This verse indicates how important it is for believers to think on the Word of God. As we do, the Lord illuminates the Word to our minds so we gain insights into it and are better able to live for Him. When this occurs, our Christian lives will evidence characteristics of a good soldier, a good athlete and a good farmer.

Chapter 11 –
Remember Jesus
Christ

Remember Jesus Christ, risen from the dead, descendant of David, according to my gospel (2:8).

THE APOSTLE PAUL had urged Timothy to go on in spite of any hardship. Paul did not paint a rosy picture of the Christian life—Timothy was to have the endurance of a soldier (v. 3-4), the discipline of an athlete (v. 5) and the diligence of a good farmer (v. 6). None of these things would earn salvation for Timothy; all of it was to be done because he already had salvation, having trusted Christ as his Savior. Timothy had experienced the grace of God, and Paul was concerned that Timothy not withhold anything in telling and teaching the Good News.

But in time of suffering it is normal to become discouraged. Realizing this, Paul wrote the words of verse 8 to encourage Timothy. Paul used the Greek present tense for the word "remember" that emphasizes continual action. Paul was concerned that Timothy keep on remembering certain truths about Christ. To have victory in suffering, it is necessary to maintain a vibrant relationship with Jesus Christ. This is possible as we remember what He did for us.

Notice specifically what Paul wanted Timothy to keep remembering that "Jesus Christ [was] risen from the dead, descendant of David, according to my gospel." In referring to Jesus Christ as "descendant of David," Paul emphasized Jesus' humanity, which He took upon Himself to present Himself to Israel as its Messiah and to die for the sin of the world. This aspect of Christ's life was filled with suffering, but it was followed by glory because He had "risen from the dead." As Timothy suffered for the sake of the gospel, he was to keep remembering Jesus Christ, who suffered for everyone. As Timothy thought about Christ's suffering and the glory that followed, he would also be reminded that God would reward him for being faithful in suffering.

In referring to Christ's resurrection, Paul used the Greek perfect tense for the word "risen." This tense refers to a past act with a continuing effect. Paul was emphasizing that Christ had been raised from the dead and was still alive.

The resurrection of Jesus Christ is central to Christianity. Other men have claimed to be God, but only Jesus Christ rose from the dead and proved His claims. The great resurrection chapter of the Bible, 1 Corinthians 15, reveals that many were eyewitnesses to Christ's resurrection, so no one needs to doubt that He rose from the dead. His resurrection assures believers that they, too, will someday rise from the dead.

Paul wrote that Christ rose from the dead "according to my gospel" (2 Tim. 2:8). This phrase emphasized that the resurrection of Christ was in full agreement with the gospel God had entrusted to him to proclaim to others. Having mentioned the gospel, Paul told of his relationship to it:

For which I suffer hardship even to imprisonment as a criminal; but the word of God is not imprisoned (2:9).

Here Paul reveals the difficulty that his relationship with the gospel had brought him. The words "suffer hardship" are translated from the word *kakopatheō*, which means "to suffer evil, endure affliction." In Bible times this word was frequently used when speaking of the hardships experienced in military service. The same basic word is used in 1:8 and

2:3.

In 2:9, Paul said he was suffering hardships "as a criminal." Apart from this verse, the Greek word Paul used for "criminal" is found only in Luke 23:32-33, 39, where it is plural and is also translated "criminals." Luke 23 refers to the criminals who were being put to death at the time Christ was crucified. So we see in 2 Timothy 2:9 that because of Paul's relationship with the gospel he was being treated as a criminal.

Paul was experiencing hardships "even to imprisonment," or literally, "even to the point of bonds." Others were suffering hardships too, but not necessarily to the extent of being in bonds as was Paul. Although his circumstances were not encouraging, Paul sounded a note of triumph when he wrote: "But the word of God is not imprisoned." Paul realized that the Roman government could put him in prison and prevent him from proclaiming the gospel to others but it could never bind God's message itself. In referring to the message as not being bound, Paul used the Greek perfect tense again. As such, Paul was saying, "The word of God has not been, and is not now, imprisoned."

This is encouraging to remember. If the believer is laid aside because of illness or has restrictions placed on him so he cannot openly proclaim the gospel, God's message is not imprisoned—it can continue to have an effect on the lives of others. Because Paul realized that no one could ever effectively bind the gospel, he said,

For this reason I endure all things for the sake of those who are chosen, so that they may also obtain the salvation which is in Christ Jesus *and* with *it* eternal glory (2:10).

This was Paul's response as he remembered Jesus Christ and the power of the gospel—he was willing to experience anything for the sake of those who would believe the gospel. The Greek word translated "endure" is made up of two Greek words literally meaning "to remain under." One endures hardship by remaining under it. Paul did not say that it was easy to do this, but he was willing to do it "for the sake of those who are chosen, so that they may also obtain the salvation which is in Christ Jesus *and* with *it* eternal glory." Because of the eternal benefits to those who receive Christ as Savior, Paul was willing to endure anything necessary to give them the opportunity to hear and believe the gospel. Because he knew the eternal results, he was willing to suffer temporal hardships.

Chapter 12 – Life Because of Death

It is a trustworthy statement: For if we died with Him, we will also live with Him (2:11).

THE FIRST PHRASE of this verse literally reads "Trustworthy is the statement," and the same expression in the original language occurs in 1 Timothy 1:15, 3:1, 4:9, and in Titus 3:8. This statement seems to introduce a quotation that had gained wide acceptance in the early Church. The quotation which follows (2 Tim. 2:11-13) is commonly considered to have been a fragment of an early hymn.

The first part of the statement, of saying, is "If we died with Him, we will also live with Him." The Greek word concerning death is *sunapothnēskō*, which is a compound word meaning "to die together" or "to die with." The word concerning life is also a compound word and means "to live together" or "to live with."

This statement in 2 Timothy 2:11 compares closely to the statement that is made in Romans 6:8: "Now if we have died with Christ, we believe that we shall also live with Him." The context of Romans 6 reveals that when a person receives Christ as his Savior, he shares in the death of Christ, and from that time onward he is spiritually alive. This is apparently the same truth Paul was emphasizing to Timothy, reminding him to remember, in the midst of suffering, that since he had died with Christ, he was living with Christ. Remembering this basic truth would bring Timothy encouragement in suffering.

Paul further stated,

If we endure, we will also reign with Him; If we deny Him, He also will deny us (2:12).

The word translated "endure" is composed to two words: *hupo*, meaning "under," and *menō*, meaning "to abide" or "to remain." To remain under difficult circumstances is "to persevere" or "to endure." The believer who perseveres in suffering is promised that he will reign with Christ. Here we see the direct correlation of eternal rewards and faithfulness in this life. This principle is seen in Matthew 25:21, where the master said to the servant, "Well done, good and faithful slave. You were faithful with a few things, I will put you in charge of many things; enter into the joy of your master."

The statement "If we deny Him, He will also deny us" is sometimes limited by Bible students to refer to salvation. Certainly, those who deny Christ by refusing to receive Him as Savior will be denied by Christ in the future. However, since the context of 2 Timothy 2 has to do with suffering for Christ, it is more probably that these words refer to the believer's denying Christ in his daily life by not being faithful to Christ or by refusing to be a good testimony for Him. Although the believer has eternal life because he has been delivered from condemnation by receiving Christ, he will also be denied rewards by Christ if he denies Christ in his daily walk. First Corinthians 3:15 tells of those believers who are denied rewards: "If any man's work is burned up, he will suffer loss; but he himself will be saved, yet so as through fire." Paul compared the Christian life to athletes competing in track and said, "Do you not know that those who run in a race all run, but *only* one receives the prize? Run in such a way that you may win" (1 Cor. 9:24). The believer who excels in this life will be richly rewarded by Christ in the next. Paul concluded the faithful saying with the words:

If we are faithless, He remains faithful, for He cannot deny

Himself (2:13).

Here again the context indicates that this verse refers to believers who are suffering for the cause of the gospel. The word translated "faithless" is *apisteō*, which means not only "disbeliever" or "refuse to believe" but also "unfaithful." Applying this statement to salvation, it is true that those who refuse to believe Christ do not negate the message of salvation or the faithfulness of Christ. But it is also true of believers, that, although they may occasionally lapse into sin and are not as faithful to the Lord as they ought to be, He is always faithful. It is impossible for the Lord to lapse in faithfulness because this would deny His own character.

Hebrews 13:8 assures us, "Jesus Christ *is* the same yesterday and today and forever." How encouraging it is to remember that even though we have lapses in faithfulness, Jesus Christ is always faithful to us.

When these truths are really grasped, they will cause the believer to be even more faithful, for he will serve Christ out of love and gratitude rather than out of fear. Christ does not expect the impossible from us. As the psalmist said, "For He Himself knows our frame; He is mindful that we are *but* dust" (Ps. 103:14). Let us rejoice in the faithfulness of God and respond as did the psalmist: "I will sing of the lovingkindness of the Lord forever; to all generations I will make known Your faithfulness with my mouth" (89:1).

Chapter 13 - Personal and Public Responsibility

Remind *them* of these things, and solemnly charge *them* in the presence of God not to wrangle about words, which is useless *and leads* to the ruin of the hearers (2:14).

HAVING TOLD TIMOTHY of life and death issues (vv. 11-13), Paul next told him to remind believers of these things. The Greek word translated "remind" is in the present tense which emphasizes continuous action. Paul was urging Timothy to keep on reminding people of these important truths.

Those who attend church tend to want to hear some new truth that will revitalize their lives. However, God is not presently giving additional revelation; the canon of Scriptures has been closed. The pastor's responsibility, therefore, is not to present previously unrevealed truth to his people but to teach them the truths already recorded in the Word of God and then to constantly remind them of these truths.

Timothy was to charge believers "not to wrangle about words, which is useless." In making this statement, Paul used a Greek word that is not found in any other place in the New Testament. The word is *logomacheō* and means "to strive with words." How deplorable it is to God for believers to have word battles. No acts may be involved, but believers can have a cold war with one another and disrupt the harmony that God intends for them to have. It is necessary to defend the faith, of course, and words are necessary to do this, but Paul referred to word battles that are "useless."

Believers must be careful not to argue over issues that are not truly important. We must make sure there is clear revelation in God's Word concerning the matter over which we make an issue. We must be careful not to argue about things that are really not important but only reflect our personality.

Notice what happens when believers have word battles about unimportant matters—it causes "the ruin of the hearers." The Greek word translated "ruin" is *katastrophē* from which the word "catastrophe" is derived. The Greek word means "to overthrow" and conveyed the idea of "turning upside down." Paul was saying that useless word battles by believers were causing some to be overthrown as they listened. Perhaps Paul was referring to young converts who became disheartened and were hindered in their spiritual growth as they heard older believers talk.

Having emphasized Timothy's responsibility in this regard, Paul told him:

Be diligent to present yourself approved to God as a workman who does not need to be ashamed, accurately handling the word of truth (2:15).

Although Timothy would have done much studying of the Scriptures and of other books, Paul referred to much more than study as we commonly think of it. The word translated "diligent" is *spousdazō* and means "to be zealous" or "to make every effort." Paul was concerned that Timothy be diligent in his desire to be approved by God. This would certainly include study as we know it, but it would especially include obedience to the truths he would learn from the Scriptures. In every area of life all believers are to make every effort to be approved by God.

Paul urged Timothy to be a "workman" (laborer) who does not need to be ashamed. The word translated "ashamed" means "to be put to shame." Paul was no doubt thinking of the future time when Timothy would give account to God for what he had done in this life. Paul wrote elsewhere concerning believers: "For we must all appear before the judgment seat of Christ, so that each one may be recompensed for his deeds in the body, according to what he has done, whether good or bad" (2 Cor. 5:10). As we give account to the Lord, we will have no need to be put to shame if we have been faithful laborers for Him. Believers are stewards of the gospel and Paul said, "In this case, moreover, it is required of stewards that one be found trustworthy" (1 Cor. 4:2). In Timothy's case, he was to be faithful not only in his personal life but also in shepherding the flock God had committed to his trust.

Paul also instructed Timothy: "accurately handling the word of truth." The Greek word translated "accurately" is *orthotomeō* which means "to cut straight." This word was used in New Testament times of cutting a straight furrow and of cutting stones by a mason. However, Paul may have taken the word from his own profession of tentmaking, in which it was necessary to cut straight from the rough camel-hair cloth. Whichever the case, from the context it is evident that Paul was concerned that Timothy properly handle the Word of God and not misuse or misinterpret it. The believer must always be careful not to twist the Scriptures to fit his own theology but rather to conform his theology to the Scriptures. Good Bible study seeks to glean all that can be derived from a given verse, but one must also be careful not to derive more than the verse actually says.

But avoid worldly *and* empty chatter, for it will lead to further ungodliness (2:16).

Positively, Timothy was to be diligent in seeking to be approved by God; negatively, he was to "avoid worldly *and* empty chatter." The word translated "worldly" means "unhallowed" and is opposite in meaning to "sacred." That which does not edify, or build up believers, is to be shunned by the Christian who wants to please Christ. Also to be avoided is "empty chatter," which literally means "empty talk." This is the kind of talk that does not contribute positive good to the believer's welfare. Paul was not suggesting that everything a believer says must be directly related to spiritual truths, but he was emphasizing that whatever is said must not dishonor the Lord. The believer's responsibility is to avoid, or shun, all conversation that dishonors the Lord.

The reason the believer should shun such chatter is because "it will lead to further ungodliness." Conversation that is dishonoring to the Lord does not tend to get better, but worse. This is why a Christian should have no part of such conversation because it cannot possibly benefit his or her relationship with the Lord nor his or her testimony to others. Each believer is responsible to heed Paul's instruction recorded in Ephesians 4:29: "Let no unwholesome word proceed from your mouth, but only such a *word* as is good for edification according to the need of *the moment*, so that it will give grace to those who hear."

Chapter 14 – God's Foundation Is Sure

PAUL WARNED TIMOTHY to "avoid worldly and empty chatter, for it will lead to further ungodliness" (2:16). Paul went on to instruct Timothy:

And their talk will spread like gangrene. Among them are Hymenaeus and Philetus (2:17).

Here Paul warned Timothy that "empty chatter" would "spread like gangrene." The word translated "spread" is *nomē* which was used of pasturing or feeding. Empty talk that dishonors the Lord eats away on a person until he has severe spiritual problems. The word translated "gangrene" is *gaggraina;* that is, it spreads like cancer.

Paul then singled out two individuals—Hymenaeus and Philetus—who were particularly responsible for vain babblings which had eaten as a gangrene in those who heard them. Although it is not possible to know for sure, Hymenaeus may be the same person to whom Paul referred in 1 Timothy 1:19-20: "Keeping faith and a good conscience, which some have rejected and suffered shipwreck in regard to their faith. Among them are Hymenaeus and Alexander, whom I have handed over to Satan, so that they will be taught not to blaspheme." Concerning Philetus, nothing further is known. However, the error of Hymenaeus and Philetus was clearly evident:

Men who have gone astray from the truth saying that the resurrection has already taken place, and they upset the faith of some (2:18).

The word "astray" is a translation of *astocheō* which means "to miss the mark." Hymenaeus and Philetus taught information that missed the mark as far as truth was concerned. They taught that "the resurrection has already taken place." Although the details of their teaching are not known, it may have been based on two impressions that seem to have been common in the first century. First, there was widespread teaching that the physical body, because it is material, is evil. This teaching was particularly promoted by the Gnostics, and it had its effect in Christian circles. Since the body is evil, according to this teaching, a Christian who believed such would have extreme difficulty thinking that God could ever resurrect the physical body. Some therefore believed that the resurrection had to do with the work of God in a person's life, not with the physical body. Even today some maintain that resurrection has to do only with God's work in a person and that it is unrelated to the physical body.

The Corinthians were apparently affected by this erroneous teaching also, for Paul dealt thoroughly with the resurrection in his first letter to them. He emphasized that the resurrection of believers is based on Christ's resurrection (15:12-23) and also that the believer's resurrection will be a physical one. Paul said of the believer's body: "It is sown a natural body, it is raised a spiritual body. If there is a natural body, there is also a spiritual *body*" (v. 44). The believer's body *will* be raised from the dead.

Also, it is possible that the teaching of Hymenaeus and Philetus arose because times were so difficult for Christians. These two men may have thought they were in the Tribulation already and had missed the Rapture of the Church. This was a teaching that was also circulating in Thessalonica, as is evident from 2 Thessalonians. One of the reasons Paul wrote 2 Thessalonians was to assure believers that they were not living in the Tribulation.

Regardless of what form the teaching of Hymenaeus and Philetus took, the result was that they overthrew, or overturned, the faith of some of the people. Their teaching which missed the mark of the truth affected others to the point where they could not cope with spiritual truths. They gave the impression that God had forgotten the believer. But Paul gave them the correct statement:

Nevertheless, the firm foundation of God stands, having this seal, "The Lord knows those who are His," and "Everyone who names the name of the Lord is to abstain from wickedness" (2:19).

Although it might have seemed to some that the foundation of truth concerning God was wavering, Paul reminded them that it "stands." The word translated "stands" is in the Greek perfect tense which indicates that the foundation has stood sure in the past and that it continues to do so.

The seal of the foundation to which Paul referred has to do with both security and purity. As to security, the seal of the foundation is that "The Lord knows those who are His." These words should have been of tremendous comfort to those who had become confused by the teaching of Hymenaeus and Philetus concerning the resurrection. The Lord had not forgotten His own after all! Those who have trusted in Christ alone for salvation never need to think that God may forget them in the out-working of His program.

As to purity, Paul said the seal of the foundation is "Everyone who names the name of the Lord is to abstain from wickedness." The word translated "abstain" is *aphistēmi*, which means "to stand off, depart from, withdraw from." The believer is to stand away from iniquity, thereby having no part in it. The one who knows Jesus Christ as Savior should desire to please Him in everything.

Let us remember in times of difficulty that God has not forgotten us and that as we seek to please Him, He will do a significant work in our lives and will use us to enrich the lives of others.

Chapter 15 - Becoming a Special Vessel

Now in a large house there are not only gold and silver vessels, but also vessels of wood and of earthenware, and some to honor and some to dishonor (2:20).

ALTHOUGH THE ENGLISH word "now," which begins this verse, shows contrast, the Greek word involved can also mean "then," simply indicating a transition. Contrast is evident in the passage because Paul does not want Timothy to become like Hymenaeus and Philetus who were teaching that the resurrection had already taken place (vv. 17-18). However, the context also indicates that Paul was simply going on in verse 20 to emphasize to Timothy—and to every believer— what is required if he wishes to be a special vessel for God.

In emphasizing his point, Paul used the analogy of a great house that has two basic kind of vessels—those of much value ("gold and silver") and those of little value ("wood and of earthenware"). Paul continued contrasting these two kinds of vessels in the words "some to honor and some to dishonor." Inasmuch, as a vessel, by itself, is neither moral nor immoral, it is evident that the word "dishonor" depicts the low value of the vessels rather than the possibility of bringing dishonor to their owners.

In interpreting verse 20, was Paul contrasting believers with unbelievers or was he contrasting dedicated believers with undedicated believers? Some interpreters point out that the local church is like a great house having both believers and unbelievers; the believer must live a life that is separated from unbelievers if he is to please God. Those who so interpret the passage refer to Hymenaeus and Philetus as the kind of people from whom the believer needs to be separated.

However, the passage itself contains no evidence that Hymenaeus and Philetus were unbelievers. True, they were false teachers, but they may have been believers who were greatly confused in their doctrinal beliefs.

Obviously, a believer should not participate in the sin of unbelievers, but he must be with them to reach them for Christ. However, those who claim to be Christians but who bring shame on the name of Christ are to be avoided by other believers (1 Cor. 5:11).

That 2 Timothy 2:20 refers to a believer's becoming a special vessel for the Lord rather than a lackadaisical Christian seems to be supported by verse 21:

Therefore, if anyone cleanses himself from these *things*, he will be a vessel for honor, sanctified, useful to the Master, prepared for every good work (2:21).

A literal vessel does not have the ability to change itself into another vessel, but illustrations are not true in every detail. Paul depicts the Christian as a vessel who can become more special. Because salvation is by faith in Christ alone and not by works, this verse seems to apply more to what a person does after salvation to live for the Lord.

The believer is to "cleanse himself from these." The Greek word translated "cleanse" means "to clean out." The believer who desires to be a vessel of special value to the Lord must keep himself clean. The pronoun "these" seems to refer to those vessels of little or no value described in verse 20 as being "of wood and of earthenware" and "some to dishonor."

The believer who wishes to excel for the Lord must keep himself uncontaminated by those who have the disease of mediocrity. This, too, implies that the believer should keep himself free from those things that cause a Christian to be lukewarm in his testimony. Such things are mentioned in verses 22 and 23.

But notice, the believer who keeps himself pure is one who is a "vessel for honor, sanctified, useful to the Master, prepared for every good work."

The believer who keeps himself pure is a special vessel to the Lord because he can be useful for the Lord's highest purpose; he is "sanctified" or "set apart" to serve the Lord. This verse emphasizes that it is the purity of the believer's life that enables him to be useful to the Lord, his Master.

Even the word for "Master" shows the dedication of the believer. The word is *despotēs*, from which the word "despot" is derived. The word stresses the Lord's undisputed ownership. The believer who seeks to please Christ in everything will recognize Him as the undisputed Master and will bring everything else into line with the lordship of Christ.

"Prepared for every good work" emphasizes readiness for any good work. This means that the believer must say no to certain things and yes to other things. Verse 22 presents both:

Now flee from youthful lusts and pursue righteousness, faith, love *and* peace, with those who call on the Lord from a pure heart (2:22).

The believer is to "flee" youthful lusts. He is not to constantly subject himself to these lusts and think that he will eventually become stronger by so doing. The word "lusts" refers to strong cravings or desires. The word can have both a good and bad meaning, as determined by the context.

"Youthful lusts" are those desires that characterize youth, such as ambition for self, impatience, and love of dispute. Another characteristic of youth is the desire to live for oneself and for the moment rather than taking others and the future into consideration. Those who live to please themselves are ones who must be spoken to as "men of flesh, as to infants in Christ" (1 Cor. 3:1). Such believers have self as lord instead of Jesus Christ. Paul told Timothy to "flee" those desires that characterize youth that would prevent him from being a special vessel for the Lord. By contrast, Paul urged Timothy to follow "righteousness, faith, love and peace."

The word "pursue" is used to show intensity. Instead of living for the pleasures of the moment, Timothy—and all who are to be special vessels for the Lord—would have to intensely pursue those things that are becoming to a Christian. Such a believer must live for eternal values rather than for temporal values.

But even in this pursuit of eternal values, there is fellowship with those who are like-minded, for Paul told Timothy to pursue these things "with those who call on the Lord from a pure heart." Notice that verse 21 says a person must "cleanse" himself and verse 22 refers to such people as having a "pure" heart.

How wonderful it is to know that our hearts are cleansed as we confess our sin to the Lord: "But if we walk in the Light as He Himself is the Light, we have fellowship with one another, and the blood of Jesus His Son cleanses us from all sin. If we confess our sins, He is faithful and righteous to forgive us our sins and to cleanse us from all unrighteousness" (1 John 1:7, 9).

Chapter 16 –
Instruction with Love

But refuse foolish and ignorant speculations, knowing they produce quarrels (2:23).

HERE, PAUL RETURNED to his charge to Timothy that he not become involved in word battles that are of no use in edifying believers. In verse 14, Paul commanded Timothy to charge believers "not to wrangle about words, which is useless *and leads* to the ruin of the hearers." In verse 16, he told Timothy to "avoid worldly *and* empty chatter, for it will lead to further ungodliness." He also stated that such babblings would "spread like gangrene" (v. 17). Now he tells Timothy to avoid questions that are "foolish and ignorant" (v. 23).

The word translated "foolish" is *mōros*, from which the word "moron" is derived. The word refers to that which is "foolish" or "stupid." Paul did not want Timothy to take any time for senseless questions because it would not be of any benefit to the one asking the question or to him as he tried to answer the question. Instead, taking time for such questions would have an adverse effect.

The word translated "ignorant" is *apaideutos*, which also means "stupid," or literally, "uneducated." Paul was certainly not advocating that Timothy refuse to answer sincere questions by those who wanted honest answers, but he was encouraging Timothy to avoid the questioning of those who refuse to study things for themselves and thus bring senseless questions to him.

The reason for Paul's advice was that such questionings "produce quarrels." Seeking to answer senseless, uneducated questionings of people who are not really serious gives birth to battles, or quarrels. Notice how Paul kept touching on the matter of quarrels. In verse 14 he told Timothy to charge people "not to wrangle about words, which is useless." Here, he said that seeking to answer "foolish and ignorant speculations" gives birth to "quarrels." No wonder Paul encouraged Timothy to avoid such situations. Paul went on to say that would only give birth to quarrels.

The Lord's bond-servant must not be quarrelsome, but be kind to all, able to teach, patient when wronged (2:24).

The word Paul used for "bond-servant" had a far different meaning than it has come to have in western culture. Paul used *doulos*, which was the common word at that time for "slave." Of course, the Christian is one who has willfully become a slave of Jesus Christ because of what Christ has done for him.

Paul had been directly addressing Timothy in telling him to avoid foolish and unlearned questions. Here he made a statement that includes every Christian—"The Lord's bond-servant must not be quarrelsome" (v. 24).

In the Greek text of verse 24, the negative "not" goes with the word *dei*, which means "necessary." As such, Paul was saying concerning a servant of the Lord that "it is not necessary for him to fight." A believer has no need to become involved in trying to answer "foolish and ignorant speculations" which only give birth to quarrels.

Rather than being involved in quarrels, the Lord's servant should "be kind to all, able to teach, patient when wronged" (v. 24).

Paul was concerned about being gentle to others. In writing to the Thessalonians, he reminded them: "But we proved to be gentle among you, as a nursing *mother* tenderly cares for her own children" (1 Thess. 2:7).

Paul's words "able to teach" (2 Tim. 2:24) refer to one who is not only able to teach but also ready to teach. Such a person has to be teachable himself. The Christian must be ready and able to communicate to others the all-important knowledge found in the Word of God. The responsibility of others is then to respond to the knowledge that has been communicated to them. The quality needed by the teacher is that of patience (v. 24). The word translated "patient" is *anexikakos*, which means "bearing evil without resentment." Evil must be endured, but it is to be endured without resentment. This will be true only as the believer keeps in mind that he himself is only a forgiven sinner. Remembering this, he will not be resentful to those who mistreat him.

With gentleness correcting those who are in opposition, if perhaps God may grant them repentance leading to the knowledge of the truth (2:25).

Gentleness is not inability to take a firm position on a matter; it is strength under control. The Greek word translated "gentleness" was used in Bible times to refer, for instance, to a wild horse that has been tamed. The believer is to be under the control of the Holy Spirit, but he is to take a strong position on what God's Word says. As emphasized by the word "gentleness," he should have an attitude of humility, courtesy, and considerateness, but this does not mean that he will be compromising in what he believes.

With his strength under control, the believer is to be "correcting those who are in opposition" (v. 25). From this we see that unbelievers, as well as carnal believers, are in reality only opposing themselves when they bring arguments against the truth of God's Word and those who are living under the control of the Holy Spirit. Unbelievers—if they pass from this life as such—will experience God's eternal judgment for their sin because they have refused to receive what Christ has done in their behalf (Rev. 20:11-15). Carnal believers will experience a loss of reward (1 Cor. 3:13-15; 2 Cor. 5:10).

A believer is to instruct those who oppose themselves "if perhaps God may grant them repentance leading to the knowledge of the truth." The word translated "repentance" basically refers to a change of mind that results in a change of behavior. If salvation is the issue, the unbeliever needs to change his mind concerning what he thinks about himself, about sin, and about Jesus Christ, who has paid the penalty for his sin. If carnality is the issue, the believer needs to change his thinking about sin, because he obviously does not see it in its true seriousness. He needs to realize that sin is more than breaking the law of God; sin is breaking the heart of God.

The word translated "knowledge" is Paul's word for "full knowledge." From the passage, it is evident that Paul had more in mind than just admitting to the truth; he has concerned that they respond to the truth.

And they may come to their senses and escape from the snare of the devil, having been held captive by him to do his will (2:26).

The words translated "come to their senses" actually means "to be sober again." Here, Paul viewed the one in the snare of the Devil as being mentally intoxicated. Only a recognition of, and response to, the truth brings a person out of the mentally intoxicated state in which the Devil has him ensnared.

The last phrase of verse 26, "having been held captive by him to do his will," has caused much debate as to its proper interpretation. The problem specifically involves the words "his will." The question is whether the pronoun "his" refers to the Devil or to God. Does the Devil take people captive by the will of God? Of course, it is recognized from the Book of Job that the Devil cannot go beyond the limits that God has established (1:12; 2:6).

The words "do his will" should literally read "unto his will." A.T. Robertson, a notable Greek authority of the past, admits there are difficulties with either view, but he prefers to take these words to refer to those "taken captive by the devil that they may come back to soberness to do the will of God." The believer shares a part in bringing the person back to soberness as he faithfully instructs what the Word of God has to say concerning sin and salvation.

Chapter 17 – The Last Days

But realize this, that in the last days difficult times will come (3:1).

THE APOSTLE PAUL reminded Timothy—and all believers—that things are going to become worse at the end of the age or in the "last days." The word translated "last" is *eschatos*, from which the word "eschatology" is derived. Eschatology is the study of the events of the last days.

There are "last days" for the Church. Age as well as "last days" for the nation of Israel. Second Timothy 3 deals with the last days of the Church Age. Although no prophecy has to be fulfilled before Christ returns for the Church, Paul warns of worsening conditions in the last days of the Church Age before Christ lifts out His believers from earth to heaven.

Paul cautioned that in the last days "difficult times" would come. "Difficult" is *chalepos*, which means "hard to bear, grievous, painful." Those who believe that conditions will become increasingly better before Christ returns for the Church are holding a view that does not agree with the Scriptures. Paul said that conditions would become worse, not better. The worsening conditions are evident from the scriptural description of what people will be like in these last times.

For men will be lovers of self, lovers of money, boastful, arrogant, revilers, disobedient to parents, ungrateful,

unholy" (3:2).

Where one's affection lies reveals what he considers to be most important. Verses 2-4 reveal where the affections of the masses will be in the last days. Paul said that men will be "lovers of self." These words are all translated from a single Greek word, *philautos*, meaning "to love oneself." This Greek word is a combination of the words "love" (*philos*) and "self" (*autos*). The same word for love is joined to other words in this passage to show what man will love in the last days.

"Lovers of money" is from *philarguros*, meaning "to love money." In the last days, materialism will be a characteristic of mankind more than ever before.

Because the center of attention is man himself, man will also be "boastful, arrogant, revilers." The unregenerate masses will have no regard for God. They will even think that all they have is due to their own efforts rather than being derived from God. Because of the tendency not to consider the views of others, those in the last days will also be "disobedient to parents," an expression of the breakdown of authority that will take place in those days. That man is ungrateful to others and to God is seem from the words "ungrateful, unholy." Those who refuse to acknowledge God will become more irreverent in their living.

Unloving, irreconcilable, malicious gossips, without self-control, brutal, haters of good (3:3).

The word "unloving" is translated from the Greek word *astorgos*. The "a" prefix serves as a negative on this word that relates to family affection, or love of kindred. The only other time this word is used in the New Testament is Romans 1:31, where it is also translated "unloving." Romans 1:31 refers to those who have rejected God and have been given up to all kinds of evil. Second Timothy 3:3 refers to those in the last days of the Church who will have no love for those in their own family. Even now we are seeing the breakdown of the home, a condition Paul said would exist in the last days.

Men will be "irreconcilable." This does not mean that a truce will be broken but that those in the last days will refuse to enter into a truce to terminate hostilities. It will be a time of never-ending feuds.

"Malicious gossips" is from *diabolos*, one of the names of Satan; he is a slanderer or false accuser. In the last days, the unbelieving masses will reflect this characteristic of the god whom they serve.

Men will also be "without self-control." They will be undisciplined; they will not restrain themselves in satisfying their passions because, having rejected God, they will see nothing more important than satisfying themselves. They will be "brutal." The Greek word involved means "savage" or "not tame." As conditions worsen in the last days, men will be like wild animals, living only to satisfy their own desires and being unconcerned about any future reckoning with God.

"Haters of good" is a translation of a single Greek word, *aphilagathos*. Here the word "love" (*philos*) is joined to another word "good" (*agathos*). The "a" prefix negates the word so that it means "not loving good." In the last times, men will be haters of good—both good standards and good people.

The believer who lives in the last days—and many believe we are now living in the last days—should not expect his message to be popular to the masses. However, God always has the ability to convict men of sin. The believer's responsibility is to share the gospel so God can use it to bring conviction. It is important, too, for the believer to have the opposite characteristics of those who have rejected God. The believer must not only know what he believes, he must live what he believes so others will see a difference and be drawn to Christ. Regardless of the difficult conditions, believers are still responsible to live holy lives. And unbelievers can still be saved from condemnation if they will trust Jesus Christ as personal Savior.

Chapter 18– A Growing Self-Centeredness

Treacherous, reckless, conceited, lovers of pleasure rather than lovers of God (3:4).

THESE CHARACTERISTICS CONTINUE Paul's list of what conditions and people will be like in the last times. First, they will be "treacherous." The original word meant literally "to give over" and is used in the New Testament only here and in Luke 6:16 and Acts 7:52. In the last times nothing will be held so precious that most will not be willing to betray trust, even if it puts the lives of others in peril.

"Reckless" comes from a word which means "to fall forward." It had a meaning of "rash, thoughtless." The word is used only here and in Acts 19:36, which records Alexander's words that the people ought "to keep calm and do nothing rash."

"Conceited" is from a word that literally means "puffed up." In the last days, many will have no regard for God, nor will they consider that they are obligated to Him in any way. They will be puffed up with a false estimate of their own importance. This is evidenced today by those who are proud of mankind's accomplishments but who fail to recognize that they have simply discovered laws that God has set in His universe.

"Lovers of pleasure rather than lovers of God." "Lovers of pleasure" is translated from one Greek word *philēdonos*, and "lovers of God" is translated from one word *philotheos*. Men will be "pleasure lovers" more than "God lovers."

Words used throughout the first four verses of 2 Timothy 3 reveal where people's affections will be in the last days. Mankind will be self-lovers (*philautos*) and money lovers (*philarguros*) (v. 2), not having loving kindred (*astorgos*) and not loving good (*aphilagathos*) (v. 3), and pleasure lovers (*philēdonos*) more than God lovers (*philotheos*) (v. 4). In the last days man's love will be self-centered rather than God-centered.

Holding to a form of godliness, although they have denied its power; Avoid such men as these (3:5).

Even though man won't acknowledge God as he should in the last days, he will refuse to admit he is a pagan and will still profess to be an adherent of Christianity. This profession, however, will be only a form of godliness. The word Paul used for "form" is *morphōsis*, which refers to the outward form or appearance. In the last days, one will not be able to tell who is a believer because the ungodly will have the outer appearance without the inner reality of godliness.

Although they will have the outward form, men will deny the "power" of godliness in the last days. The word translated "power" is *dunamis*—power in the sense of ability. Christ told the disciples they would receive this power, or ability, when the Holy Spirit came on the Day of Pentecost (Acts 1:8). It was with this power of the Holy Spirit, and not of man's wisdom, that Paul reminded the Corinthians he had come to them (1 Cor. 2:4-5). In the last days, however, people will appear to be godly but will not have the power which comes from God because they will not know Jesus Christ as their personal Savior.

How is the believer to respond to such people? Paul wrote: "Avoid such men as these" (2 Tim. 3:5). He used the Greek present tense, which emphasizes continuous action. The command was to "keep avoiding" such people.

For among them are those who enter into households and captivate weak women weighed down with sins, led on by various impulses (3:6).

The word translated "enter" has the meaning "to slip in by insinuation." Jude 1:4 uses this word in reference to those who "crept in unnoticed."

"They who enter" is a translation of the present participle and again represents the Greek present tense, emphasizing continuous action. The participle was used to designate an individual by his action. For instance, John the Baptist was known because of his baptizing, so he was referred to by a participial form meaning "the baptizing one." This form has carried over into English as "the Baptist."

Paul said that in the last days there would be persons whose very activity or occupation would be "creeping into houses" unaware to do as Paul described—"captivate weak women."

"Captivate" is also a present participle. Just as these men continue to creep into women's houses, they continue to lead them captive.

The women are "weak." This word is from the word *gunaikarion*, a diminutive of *gunē*, "women." The diminutive means "little women" and also had the meaning of "idle women." Some Bible scholars think the word *gunē* is used contemptuously here to mean "society ladies" or women, filled with curiosity, who are taken in by evil persons who make a profession of victimizing them.

These women are "weighed down with sins, led on by various impulses" (v. 6). Literally this means "Having been laden with sins, having been led away with various desires." Both "weighed down" and "led on" are perfect participles and, as such, reveal that both conditions existed before the creeping in and taking captive took place. And because these women have been led away by their desires, they are vulnerable to unscrupulous and immoral persons who would capitalize on these desires and make the women their servants.

Such women are those who are:

Always learning and never able to come to the knowledge of the truth (3:7).

This is a pathetic picture not only of these women but also of all persons in the last days who refuse to recognize anything as absolute truth. The intellectual elite today are no different from these women, for many of those who staff our universities are members of the elite, social or political vanguard, who cling resolutely to the proposition that it is impossible to know what truth really is. No phrase describes them better than: "Always learning, and never able to come to the knowledge of the truth." In His high priestly prayer, Jesus said, "Your word is truth" (John 17:17).

Those who refuse to recognize God's Word, the Bible, as truth, leave themselves open to be led into all kinds of perversion by those who appeal to their base desires and to their fallen intelligence.

Chapter 19– Reprobate Men; A Faithful Lord

Just as Jannes and Jambres opposed Moses, so these *men* also oppose the truth, men of depraved mind, rejected in regard to the faith (3:8).

PAUL HAD WARNED of those who "enter into households and captivate weak women" (v. 6). In verse 8 he drew an analogy between them and Jannes and Jambres. These two names were apparently part of Jewish tradition as it related to those who withstood Moses when he appeared before Pharaoh (Se Ex. 7 and 8). Although Paul probably took the names from Jewish tradition, the Holy Spirit superintended so he did not select erroneous details from this tradition.

Just as Jannes and Jambres withstood Moses, Paul pointed out, so those resist the truth who enter into households and lead women captive. The word "oppose" in verse 8 is translated from the word, *anthistēmi*. This word means "to set oneself against, withstand." Such people have a form of godliness but deny the power of it (v. 5).

Paul said they were men of "depraved" minds. The Greek tense of the word translated "depraved" indicates that this corrupting had taken place in the past and that its effect had continued to the present.

Because their minds had become depraved, they were reprobate concerning the faith. The word translated "rejected" is *kataphtheirō*. The word was used in New Testament times to describe that which was damaged or injured. The individuals referred to in 2 Timothy 3:8, were spiritually damaged or injured because of minds that had become depraved.

But they will not make further progress; for their folly will be obvious to all, just as Jannes's and Jambres's folly was also (3:9).

In this verse, Paul indicated that those who pursue the course of action taken by those men will eventually be exposed to everyone. In this context, they had already made inroads into the thinking of others, but Paul said they would proceed no further because their "folly" would be evident to everyone.

The word translated "folly" is *anoia*, which refers to human ignorance or lack of good sense. Paul said that this lack would be evident to all—not just to believers. By the words "was also" Paul indicated that the human ignorance of Jannes and Jambres was also revealed to everyone. Pharaoh and his people finally had to admit that God was victorious over every obstacle.

Now you followed my teaching, conduct, purpose, faith, patience, love, perseverance (3:10).

This verse and verse 11 served as a reminder of the past as Paul wrote to Timothy. Timothy had faithfully followed Paul ever since Paul had come to Derbe and Lystra and had made Timothy his disciple (Acts 16:1-5). The reference to Timothy is emphatic in 2 Timothy 3:10, for it literally reads: "But you, you followed." Timothy stands in sharp contrast to those referred to in the previous verses who did not follow correct teaching.

Each of the nine items mentioned in verses 10 and 11 has a definite article (the), indicating they all fit the pattern of the first mentioned: "my teaching." Each of these was related to Paul. No doubt, the order in which Paul listed them was also significant. On this teaching Paul had based his life; hence, "conduct." The list is continued into verse 11:

Persecutions, *and* sufferings, such as happened to me at Antioch, at Iconium *and* at Lystra; what persecutions I endured, and out of them all the Lord rescued me (3:11)!

Timothy would have been aware of these things mentioned by Paul, particularly those things that happened to Paul at Lystra, since this was Timothy's hometown. The Book of Acts tells what happened to Paul at Antioch in Pisidia (13:14-52), Iconium (14:1-5) and Lystra (14:6-19).

Having listed these items for Timothy, Paul added: "What persecutions I endured." The list refers to the persecutions that Paul had endured, but he was not content simply to tell of these; he gave credit to the Lord—"and out of them all the Lord rescued me!"

In this clause, Paul constructed the words in a way that would place the emphasis on the Lord. Paul did not want others to focus attention on him because of what he had endured but on the Lord for having delivered him. What a significant principle in testifying for the Lord; what the believer experiences is secondary to what the Lord has done for him. The best testimony is that which focuses attention on the Lord, not on the believer.

Chapter 20 - Willing to Suffer

Indeed, all who desire to live godly in Christ Jesus will be persecuted (3:12).

HAVING TOLD OF the persecutions that he had endured, Paul did not want Timothy to think that only he had suffered in this way. He assured Timothy that such suffering would be experienced by everyone who lives a godly life.

The words "all who desire" are directed specifically at those Christians who determine to live godly lives. Notice that a godly life is not just a product of the intellect. The accumulation of information does not, in itself, produce godliness. Neither is godliness the product of just the emotions; it is not enough for one to feel he ought to please God by the way he lives. Godliness does involve the intellect and the emotions, but it particularly centers in the will. A believer must choose to obey God and choose to reject the temptations of the world, the flesh and the Devil.

Obedience to God's truth causes the believer to be set apart, or sanctified, in daily living. The Apostle Peter told believers, "Since you have in obedience to the truth purified your souls for a sincere love of the brethren, fervently love one another from the heart (1 Pet. 1:22). By an act of the will, a believer is to choose to obey the truth of God that results in a purity of life. In its simplest form, this means saying yes to Christ and no to sin.

In writing to Timothy, Paul emphasized the position that each believer has by referring to those who "live godly in Christ Jesus." In Paul's view, the believer's source and enablement for a pure life is not in himself but in Christ, who provides all that the believer needs. Christ provides not only freedom from the penalty of sin but also victory over the power of sin.

Paul said that all who live godly lives in Christ Jesus "will be persecuted." The persecution would not necessarily be the same kind that Paul suffered. Those who determine to live godly lives discover that persecution takes various forms. Some Christians have been martyrs for the faith, but others have found that persecution can come in the form of social pressure and rejection by their contemporaries because of their faith. To still other well-qualified Christians, it has meant that the academic community has rejected them in their field of study. Others have been passed over for promotions in business because top management doesn't care to promote one who refuses to compromise his principles if management thinks he should. Although the persecution takes various forms and is more intense at certain times, it is inescapable that all who determine to live godly lives will suffer persecution.

But evil men and imposters will proceed *from bad* to worse, deceiving and being deceived (3:13).

The "but" of verse 13 contrasts the ungodly (evil men and imposters) with the godly (v. 12). The ungodly increase in wickedness whereas the godly continue to be persecuted.

The phrase "evil men" in verse 13 seems to refer to those described in verses 2-5. The word "imposters" in the same verse points to those outlined in verses 6-9. The word translated "imposter" is *goēs* which means "swindler." This word appears only here in the New Testament. Paul did not paint an encouraging picture; he wrote that evil men and imposters will continue to increase in wickedness.

The words translated "will proceed" is *prokoptō*, which means "go forward" or "advance." In this verse, it is not an advance of good but an increase in degeneracy.

Not only will these evil men and imposters deceive others, they will be deceived themselves—"deceiving and being deceived." Such men have rejected the truths set forth in God's Word and hold to no absolute truth. As a result, they are able to deceive others. But because they have no absolute standards, they deceive themselves.

This verse reveals that mankind is not improving, even though the environment has been revitalized. Men's degeneracy goes from bad to worse regardless of his environment. Some look at this passage and reason that if things keep getting progressively worse in the end times, there is no use in resisting evil. Paul anticipated such thinking and answered it in the following verse:

You, however, continue in the things you have learned and become convinced of, knowing from whom you have learned *them* (3:14).

The "however" of this verse contrasts Timothy with evil men and imposters. Even though others would become increasingly more degenerate, Paul emphasized that it was Timothy's personal responsibility to continue in the things that he had learned and had been assured of. The word translated "continue" is *menō*, which means "remain" or "abide." Timothy was to keep his feet firmly planted in the truths he had been taught.

The things to which Paul referred are the truths of God's Word, as is evident from the Scriptures. Paul reminded Timothy that he had "learned" these things. There had been instruction—information, that had been communicated to Timothy. But it was more than information, for he had been "convinced of" these things.

The word translated "convinced of" is *pistoō*, which means "feel confidence." As Timothy gained information from the

Word, he became convinced that these things were true. However, one must realize that these things were true whether or not Timothy became convinced of them. Today, some determine truth by experience; they don't even accept passages in the Bible as being true if those passages don't agree with their experiences. But the Bible is God's revelation of Himself and is true whether or not man accepts it. Timothy had accepted the truth of God's Word, and Paul reminded him of this fact and of his responsibility to continue in the things that he had learned.

Paul reminded Timothy: "knowing from whom you have learned *them*." Included in this group would be the Old Testament prophets, but more specifically, the Apostle Paul himself and Timothy's mother and grandmother, Eunice and Lois (1:5). Then Paul called particular attention to the character of those who had communicated God's truths to Timothy. Such people were not out for personal gain, as were the evil men and imposters; instead, they were concerned about Timothy's eternal welfare.

A characteristic of false teachers is that they are especially anxious to win converts to their cause for personal gain. As the believer witnesses to the truth of God's Word, he needs to express his concern for the unbeliever. The unbeliever must be helped to realize that the message being given is for his benefit alone—not that the believer gains something if the unbeliever responds to the message.

Chapter 21- Source for Equipping Believers

And that from childhood you have known the sacred writings which are able to give you the wisdom that leads to salvation through faith which is in Christ Jesus (3:15).

HERE PAUL REMINDED Timothy of the great benefit he had received by being taught the Scriptures from earliest childhood. The word Paul used for "childhood" was *brephos*. Although this word was used even of a baby in the womb (Luke 1:41, 44), here Paul was stressing that Timothy had been taught the Scriptures from earliest childhood.

Only the Old Testament Scriptures were available during Timothy's early childhood. The word translated "sacred writings" is *gramma*, meaning "letter" (of the alphabet) or "document" or "piece of writing." From earliest childhood, Timothy had learned from the holy letters of the Old Testament Scriptures. No doubt his mother, Eunice, had used these Scriptures to teach Timothy to read and write as well as to teach him the commands and principles they revealed. Such a close acquaintance with the Old Testament writings had a significant influence on Timothy's life.

Paul reminded Timothy that the Old Testament Scriptures were "able to give you the wisdom that leads to salvation." The Scriptures were not meant just to communicate information but to bring a person to a right relationship with God—the Author of the Scriptures. Since they were the only ones available in Timothy's youth, Paul's statement indicates that he considered the Old Testament Scriptures to be clear in its teaching of salvation.

The means of salvation is emphasized by the words "through faith which is in Christ Jesus." Even in Old Testament times, salvation was not by works but by faith. Romans 4 reveals that Abraham, who lived before the Law, and David, who lived during the time of the Law, were both saved by faith. Even though the Old Testament Scriptures did not communicate much information about Jesus Christ, these Scriptures looked forward to the time when the Lamb of God would come to take away the sin of the world. John the Baptist recognized Jesus Christ to be this Lamb of God (John 1:29). With the clear revelation of the New Testament concerning Jesus Christ's death, burial and resurrection, we now look back at the time when He offered Himself for sin, to provide salvation.

Having referred to what Timothy had gained from the Scriptures, Paul then stated what is considered a classic passage on the inspiration of the Scriptures:

All Scripture is inspired by God and profitable for teaching, for reproof, for correction, for training in righteousness (3:16).

This passage does not discuss various views of inspiration; rather, it asserts simply that "all Scripture is inspired by God." The word translated "all" can also be translated "every" in referring to the writings at the time that had been given by inspiration. The word Paul used for "Scripture" in verse 16 is different than the one used in verse 15. *Gramma* is used in verse 15 to emphasize the written characteristics, whereas *graphē*, meaning "writing" is used in verse 16. In the New Testament, *graphē* always refers to the Holy Scriptures.

Paul said that this Scripture was "inspired by God." These words are translated from *theopneustos*, which is a combination of two words meaning, literally, "God-breathed." The holy writings were given by God through human authors, who penned the precise words that God desired them to select. God did not override the personalities or wills of the human authors. Rather, God worked through them in such a way that their personalities were preserved in the writings and yet a record was produced that was without error. Some maintain that only the concepts, or ideas, are inspired by God but not the words themselves. However, apart from the words of the holy writings, there can be no absolutely authoritative thoughts or concepts. To change a given word is to change the precise concept. Inspiration is not claimed for copies of the originals or for translations into other languages. Although the original manuscripts do not exist today, gifted scholars have diligently compared the readings of the available manuscripts so that little doubt remains as to what the original manuscripts contained.

Because the Scriptures are inspired by God, they are "profitable for teaching, for reproof, for correction, for training in righteousness." The word used for "profitable" is *ōphelimos*, meaning "useful, beneficial, advantageous" and appear only here and in 1 Timothy 4:8 and Titus 3:8.

First, the inspired Scripture is beneficial for "teaching." All one needs to be taught concerning his relationship with God is revealed in the inspired Scriptures. Obeying this teaching will also enable a person to be in a right relationship with other people.

Second, Scripture is profitable for "reproof." Because Scripture is inspired by God, it is truth (John 17:17), and it is to be used to refute falsehoods. Only the Scriptures specifically reveal truths about God. From nature, one can see that God must exist (Rom. 1:20), but God has revealed specific truths about Himself only in the Scriptures.

Third, Scripture is beneficial for "correction." The word involved is *epanorthōsin*, which means "correcting, improvement." The word is composed of three different Greek words, literally meaning "to straighten up." When seeking to correct others, whether they are believers or unbelievers, the Scriptures provide the only safe guidance.

What really counts is not an individual's personal view, but God's evaluation of a situation. In restoring one to an upright state, one must first decide what such a state is. The Scriptures reveal God's standards and give guidance in such matters.

Fourth, because all Scripture is God-breathed, it is beneficial for "training in righteousness." The word translated "training" is *paideia*, meaning "training, discipline." Just as a child is trained and disciplined, so the Scriptures are of value and training and disciplining the believer in all righteous living. This same Greek word is translated "discipline" in Ephesians 6:4 and Hebrews 12:5,7-8,11. As the Word of God is studied and applied to an individual's life, it enables him to live righteously.

So that the man of God may be adequate, equipped for every good work (3:17).

This verse states the results accomplished by the Scriptures in the life of the believer. The intent is that the man of God may be "adequate." The word translated adequate is *artios* and means "complete, capable, efficient." The word does not imply that there are no imperfections in the individual. This is the only time this word appears in the New Testament. Vincent says that the idea of *artios* is that of "mutual, symmetrical adjustment of all that goes to make the man; harmonious combination of different qualities and powers."

That which especially equips the believer to do the work God intends for him is the Scriptures. Other fields of study many contribute to his well-being in life, but only the Scriptures effectively equip him for the job God has for him to do. The believer, who is so equipped by reading and obeying the Word, is "equipped for every good work." The word "equipped" is translated from the Greek word, *exartizō*. This word is related to *artios*, but with the added preposition, *ex*, it has the sense of "altogether fit" or "fully fitted."

From this we see that the Scriptures lack nothing in preparing the believer to do "every good work."

Although it is not specifically stated what is meant by all, or every, good work, the implication from the context is that the good work is done by using the Scriptures "for teaching, for reproof, for correction, for training in righteousness" (v. 16). As every believer—not just the professional minister—is equipped with the Scriptures, he is fully fitted to teach, refute, correct and educate in the area of man's most basic need—his relationship with God.

Chapter 22– Five Imperatives for Sound Doctrine

I solemnly charge *you* in the presence of God and of Christ Jesus, who is to judge the living and the dead, and by His appearing and His kingdom (4:1).

IN THIS LAST chapter of his last letter, the Apostle Paul packed his conclusion with emotion as he gave final instructions and appeals to Timothy and also told that he was ready to meet the Lord.

In the first four verses of chapter 4, Paul emphasized to Timothy the solemnity of the charge (v. 1), stated the charge (v. 2) and gave the reasons for the charge (vv. 3-4).

The word "charge" (v. 1) is a translation of *diamarturomai*, meaning "charge, warn, adjure." In secular Greek, this word was used to call the gods and men to witness. It was used in such expressions as "I adjure you."

The witnesses Paul was calling were not the pagan gods, however, but the true God: "I charge you in the presence of God and of Christ Jesus." It was a serious enough matter for the apostle to give a charge to Timothy, but Paul made it even more grave by emphasizing that the charge was being made in the presence of God.

The older manuscripts do not have the word "Lord" in this verse in connection with Christ Jesus. In addition, it is significant to realize the "and" (*kai*) can also be translated "even." Paul may well have been citing the deity of Jesus Christ because the phrase could be translated "before God, even Jesus Christ." Paul wrote "Christ Jesus," a form of the name he used often.

Having referred to Jesus Christ, Paul emphasized the solemnity of the charge to Timothy by telling what Christ would do: "who is to judge the living and the dead, and by His appearing and His kingdom." A person's words are taken seriously when one realizes he must give account to Jesus Christ, who is the Judge of all. The words "who is to judge" are literally "the one about to judge." Paul expected the Lord's coming, and he did not consider it a long time before Jesus Christ would begin His judging work of "the living and the dead."

As Paul looked ahead to Christ's coming, he realized that both those who were alive when He came and those who had died before His coming would be judged by Him. At this point, Paul did not seem to be so concerned about distinguishing between the time of these judgments as he was concerned about stressing the fact that everyone will eventually stand before Him to give account.

The phrase "and by His appearing and His kingdom" reveals Paul's belief in the personal, visible return of Jesus Christ to establish His rule on earth. Although unbelievers may ignore God or even teach false concepts of God, all may be assured that Jesus Christ is going to return and that each one will have to give an account before Him.

Those who have trusted him as Savior will give account and be rewarded for what they have done for Christ in this life (2 Cor. 5:10). Those who have not received Him as Savior will stand before the Great White Throne to give account and will be confined to the lake of fire for rejecting Christ as Savior (Rev. 20:11-15). Because the coming of Christ is sure, believers must proclaim what the world so desperately needs in order to be ready to meet Him. This is why Paul told Timothy:

Preach the word; be ready in season and out of season; reprove, rebuke, exhort, with great patience and instruction (4:2).

In this verse, Paul stated his charge to Timothy with five imperatives; no doubt the first is the most significant because it is the basis for the rest: "Preach the word." Although the word "preach" causes many to think of the professional minister, this was not what Paul was thinking. The word he used was *kerussō*, meaning "to proclaim" or "to announce."

Those in the Roman Empire of Paul's day would have been acquainted with this word because it was used of the imperial herald, who represented the emperor and who proclaimed in an authoritative manner what the emperor wanted all to hear. So too, Timothy's responsibility—and that of all believers today—was to authoritatively proclaim the message that God has given so that all could know what was required if they were to be in right relationship with God. The imperatives of verse 2 are in the aorist tense, which emphasizes urgency. Urgency is required not only because of the need of those to whom the message is to be proclaimed, but also because Jesus Christ may return at any time.

Notice that the believer is not to preach moral reform—although he ought to be interested in improving society. The believer's concern is to give the message from God that will not only help for the present time but also for eternity. Man's most basic need is to be able to live in right relationship with God for only then will he be able to live in right relationship with others. Only as the Word is proclaimed can others see the need to trust Christ as Savior and to live a life that pleases Him.

Paul also charged Timothy: "Be ready in season *and* out of season." The meaning of the word translated "ready" is "stand by." It does not imply being quick, but refers to being prepared at any time. "In season" is the convenient time; "out of season" is the inconvenient time. But Paul stressed that the believer is to be ready to proclaim the message of God whether the time is convenient or not.

Believers have undoubtedly failed most in their witnessing because they have waited for a convenient time or the right situation before they spoke a word for the Lord. The believer is to be constantly prepared so that on a moment's notice he can give God's message to others. It does not need to be a formal presentation, but it is important that each believer clearly understand the gospel so he can share it with someone else. As we are prepared to speak at any time, we will find that more opportunities arise than we expected.

Paul's third imperative to Timothy was to "reprove." The word Paul used means "to bring to light," or "to convince." The message is to be given so that, even if others don't agree with it, they are convinced of their need of Jesus Christ. The Holy Spirit will use the Word to convince people of their sin and of the need to know Christ as Savior (John 16:8). God's Word, not our word, produces true conviction of sin and of the need for salvation. Yet, God has chosen believers as the means by which He wants His Word to be expressed.

Paul's fourth imperative to Timothy was "rebuke." The word Paul used was *epitimaō* meaning "to censor" or "to warn." Whereas "reprove" seems to refer to convincing unbelievers, "rebuke" seems to refer to correcting or warning believers concerning behavior that is not pleasing to God. Here again, God's Word must be the basis for any censure, not the opinion of an individual believer.

Paul's fifth imperative to Timothy was to "exhort." This word is from *parakaleō* meaning "to appeal, to encourage." This Greek word is made up of *para* (alongside of) and *kaleō* (to call) and thus literally means "one called alongside to help." The noun forms of this word are used concerning the Holy Spirit and is translated "Helper" in John 14:16. It is used of Jesus Christ and is translated "Advocate" in 1 John 2:1. A believer is to exhort other believers—he is to consider himself as one called alongside to help and encourage other believers in their walk with the Lord. Sometimes this may involve correction, but usually it will involve comfort and encouragement.

The last phrase of verse 2, "with great patience and instruction," goes with all five imperatives Paul listed—preach, be instant, reprove, rebuke, exhort. All of these are to be done "with great patience and instruction." "Patience" refers to "endurance." The believer is not to be impatient as he works with others.

The word translated "patience" is *makrothumia*, which also appears in Galatians 5:22 as part of the fruit of the Spirit. Not only did Paul intend Timothy to evidence this fruit of the Spirit as he worked with others, but he also intended for him to use instruction as the basis for all he did. The word "instruction" comes from *didachē*, meaning "teaching." The teaching of God's Word is instruction. Here again we see that it is not the opinions of a believer but the teaching of the Word of God that is to be the basis of ministering to others.

The reason for Paul's charge to Timothy is given in verses 3 and 4:

For the time will come when they will not endure sound doctrine; but wanting to have their ears tickled, they will accumulate for themselves teachers in accordance to their own desires (4:3).

Believers are to be ready at any time to proclaim the Word (v. 2) because the time will come when people will no longer listen to the Word. The word translated "endure" means "to put up with" or "to bear with." People come to a point when they refuse to listen to "sound doctrine." The word "sound" has the meaning of "healthy." Instead of being open to the teaching of God's Word, they are open to teaching that brings a false sense of comfort.

Paul said that those who are no longer open to the Word are those who are "wanting to have their ears tickled, they will accumulate for themselves teachers in accordance to their own desires." The ones who have the itching ears are not the teachers but those who are no longer open to sound teaching of God's Word. According to their own "desires" they accumulate to themselves teachers who tell them what they like to hear.

No doubt this is the reason some prefer liberal theology, which emphasizes the false concepts that man is innately good and that all he needs to do is recognize that God loves him. But the Scriptures reveal that man has a sin nature and that the only way he can come into a right relationship with God is by trusting Jesus Christ as personal Savior. This truth does not sooth itching ears, because it emphasizes man's corruptness. Paul further described what people do when they reject God's Word:

And will turn away their ears from the truth and will turn aside to myths (4:4).

Seeking only thoughts that are comforting, such people reject the truth of God's Word and accept "myths." These persons live in a dream world because they are not being honest with themselves about their own sinful condition, nor are they honest with God in admitting that His Word is truth.

Those who turn from the truth of God's Word to myths eventually take the position that even God's Word is a myth. Individuals of liberal theological persuasion do not accept the persons and events of the early chapters of the Bible to be historically valid. They think these persons and events are only myths that merely represent certain truths.

Such a view is contrary to what the Lord Jesus Christ proclaimed when He was on the earth. His statements revealed that He believed the persons of the early chapters of Genesis to be real persons and the events to be real events. He referred to the beginning, when man was created "male and female" (Matt. 19:4). He also recognized that Noah lived at a specific time because of His reference to the days of Noah (Matt. 24:37).

Paul's statement's to Timothy about those who reject the truth and accept myths have been true of some individuals in every area. It has been increasingly true, however, as time advances and the last days come upon the Church. Paul's statement in 2 Timothy 3:7 is applicable to these people: "always learning and never able to come to the knowledge of the truth." Knowing that people will turn from the truth, a believer's responsibility is to use every opportunity to communicate the truth of God's Word to others before this takes place.

Chapter 23– Running the Race

But you, be sober in all things, endure hardship, do the work of an evangelist, fulfill your ministry (4:5).

IN CONTRAST TO those who turn from the sound doctrine and want their ears tickled with soothing thoughts, Paul commanded Timothy: "be sober in all things." The word translated "sober" is *nēphō*, which means "well-balanced, self-controlled." The word was used literally of one who abstained from strong drink; here it is used to emphasize Timothy's need for clarity of mind and sound judgment.

It was tremendously important that Timothy not be preoccupied with the fables and opinions of the false teachers (v. 3). Paul's command to Timothy to be sober is a present imperative, which emphasizes continuous action. Paul was telling Timothy, in essence, "Make it a practice to be sober," or "be continuously sober." There was never to be a letup in the sobriety required of Timothy.

Paul followed this command with three imperatives that indicated how Timothy was to express his soberness. First, he was to "endure hardship." This is a translation of one word, *kakopatheō*, which Paul had used previously in his second letter to Timothy. The word means "to suffer evil, or endure affliction." Another form of the word appears in 1:8, where Paul told Timothy, "join with *me* in suffering for the gospel." This form also appears in 2:3, where Paul charged Timothy to "suffer hardship with *me*, as a good soldier of Christ Jesus."

In 4:5 Paul was instructing Timothy about how he was to express his clarity of mind in all things. From this word we see that Paul was not indicating that the Christian life would be easy.

Paul also commanded Timothy, "Do the work of an evangelist." Careful observation here reveals that Paul was not commanding Timothy to be an evangelist but only to do the work of an evangelist. Some have the spiritual gift of evangelism, as indicated in Ephesians 4:11. Timothy's gift was probably that of pastor-teacher, as shown in the same verse. However, even though a believer does not have the gift or position of an evangelist, he is to do the work of an evangelist. That is, he is to proclaim the gospel to the lost and make the issues of sin and salvation crystal clear. He is to do this so all may know that there is forgiveness of sin and eternal life by trusting Christ as Savior. The primary work of a pastor-teacher is that of building up in the faith those who have already trusted Christ, but the message of salvation to the lost must not be omitted.

Paul further commanded Timothy, "Fulfill your ministry." The words "fulfill" are *plērophoreō*, meaning "to fill completely." Paul was concerned that nothing be lacking in Timothy's ministry. He wanted Timothy to carry out his ministry to its fullest. This would be further evidence of Timothy's continual soberness.

For I am already being poured out as a drink offering, and the time of my departure has come (4:6).

Verse 5 emphasized what Timothy was to be like in contrast to those who turn away from the truth (v. 4). In verse 6, Paul contrasted himself with Timothy. A large segment of Timothy's ministry was still future, but Paul looked on his own ministry as being at its end.

When Paul said, "I am already being poured out as a drink offering," the word he used for "offering" was *spendō*, which was used in referring to offering a libation or drink offering.

Paul viewed his own life as parallel to a drink offering that is presented to the Lord. In the Old Testament, the Israelites were instructed, "And you shall prepare wine for the drink offering, one-fourth of a hin, with the burnt offering or for the sacrifice, for each lamb. And for the drink offering you shall offer one-third of a hin of wine as a soothing aroma to the Lord" (Num. 15:5, 7). As the Apostle Paul now considered the conclusion of his life on earth, he saw it as a libation, or drink offering, which formed the last part of the sacrificial ceremony.

Paul did not view his approaching death as a failure in God's program but as a means of honoring the Lord. From John 21:19, it is evident that even the believer's death glorifies the Lord. Physical death was not the end as far as Paul was concerned; it was the beginning because it would usher him into the very presence of Jesus Christ.

Paul also added, "And the time of my departure has come" (v. 6). The word Paul used for "departure" was also used of taking down a tent, of a departure of an army and of a ship hoisting anchor in preparation for sailing. Paul used the verb form of this same word in Philippians 1:23: "But I am hard-pressed from both directions, having the desire to depart and be with Christ, for *that* is very much better."

Paul realized that his departure "has come"—ready to occur at any time. As Paul wrote from prison, he expected the Roman soldiers to come at any time to lead him off to his death. Yet, because his hope was centered on Jesus Christ, he was not wallowing in despair but was thinking of the victory that had been accomplished. This is evident from the following verse:

I have fought the good fight, I have finished the course, I have kept the faith (4:7).

As Paul looked back over his life, he compared it to those of the Greek athletes of his day. This was a favorite analogy of Paul's. He referred to such in 1 Corinthians 9:24-27, and he made reference to striving and conflict (terms of the Greek games) in Philippians 1:27, 30 and Colossians 1:29.

Paul was not boasting when he said, "I have fought the good fight." In the Greek text, the personal pronoun is not first in the sentence; it is literally "the good fight I have fought." The definite article appears in the original text: "*the* good fight." Paul viewed the Christian life as a great contest and said that he had already contested in it.

Not only had Paul finished the contest as a wrestler but he had also finished his course as a runner, for he said, "I have finished the course." When Paul addressed the Ephesian elders, he used the same terminology: "But I do not consider my life of any account as dear to myself, so that I may finish my course and the ministry which I received from the Lord Jesus, to testify solemnly of the gospel of the grace of God" (Acts 20:24). When Paul addressed these elders, he looked at the task yet before him as a runner beginning a race. In 2 Timothy, he viewed himself as having completed that course and as standing at the finish line looking back over the route.

Paul also added, "I have kept the faith." Although this can refer to the deposit of truth concerning Jesus Christ which God had entrusted to Paul, it is also possible that Paul was still drawing analogies to the Greek games. Before participating in the Greek games, an athlete had to take an oath stating that he had been in training a certain number of months and that he would not break the rules while participating in the games. With this in mind, Paul was probably emphasizing that just as he had trusted Jesus Christ as Savior and had committed his life to Him, he had also been faithful in keeping his word throughout his lifetime.

In 2 Timothy 2:5, Paul drew the analogy between the Greek contest and the Christian life in saying that a person must keep the rules if he is going to win the prize: "Also if anyone competes as an athlete, he does not win the prize unless he competes according to the rules." Because of Paul's faithfulness, he could look forward to receiving a prize.

In the future there is laid up for me the crown of righteousness, which the Lord, the righteous Judge, will award to me on that day; and not only me, but also to all who have loved His appearing (4:8).

Here, Paul continued his analogy of the Greek games and the Christian life. The Greek athlete who won the contest was given a laurel wreath by the judge. Because Paul had been faithful to God's calling, he looked ahead with assurance, knowing that he would receive "the crown of righteousness." This does not mean that Paul expected to receive righteousness as a crown, for he realized he already possessed the imputed righteousness of Christ. Earlier, Paul had written, "He made Him who knew no sin *to be* sin on our behalf, so that we might become the righteousness of God in Him" (2 Cor. 5:21).

What Paul looked forward to receiving was the reward for righteousness. And notice from whom he expected to receive the reward: "which the Lord, the righteous Judge, will award to me on that day." The Lord Jesus Christ Himself would be extending the reward to Paul for having fought the good fight, for having finished his course and for having kept the faith. Although the decisions of earthly judges can be disputed, Paul knew there would be no dispute in this case because the Lord is "the righteous Judge." In addition to drawing an analogy to the judges in the Greek games, Paul may have been thinking in particular about a judge or judges who presided over his trial.

Although in the Greek games only the first-place winner received a prize, Paul saw more than just himself receiving the crown of righteousness. Paul said, "And not only to me, but also to all who have loved His appearing." This phrase reads literally, "All those who have been loving his appearing." Notice that more is involved than just loving Christ as a person; it involves loving all He does and, in particular, loving the time when He appears for His own. A consciousness of the Lord's eventual appearing to catch away believers from the earth produces a purity of life, as 1 John 3:2-3 reveals: "Beloved, now we are children of God, and it has not appeared as yet what we will be. We know that when He appears, we will be like Him, because we will see Him just as He is. And everyone who has this hope *fixed* on Him purifies himself, just as He is pure."

How important it is that we, like Paul, might be able to look back over our lives with a sense of spiritual accomplishment and then look forward to the reward that Jesus Christ is going to present for such faithfulness.

Chapter 24- Paul Expresses Loneliness, Gives Instruction

Make every effort to come to me soon (4:9).

IN PENNING VERSE 8, Paul ended the main content of his second letter to Timothy. Verses 9-22 contain special instructions and various matters of a more personal nature.

Verse 9 reveals Paul's continuing desire to see Timothy. As Paul began his letter, he told Timothy how much he desired to see him so that he might be filled with joy (1:4).

The urgency that Paul felt as he concluded his letter is demonstrated by the Greek words and tenses he used as he wrote. The words "make every effort," are translated from *spoudao*, which means "to hurry," or 'to hasten." In addition to the meaning of the word itself, Paul used the aorist tense as he formed this imperative. In commands, this tense emphasizes urgency, Paul further emphasized the urgency by telling Timothy to come "soon." Before Paul concluded his letter, he returned to the same subject and said, "Make every effort to come before winter" (v. 21).

No doubt one of the reasons Paul longed to see Timothy was for the personal fellowship he could enjoy with him. Paul and Timothy had labored together under extreme circumstances, and the apostle was anxious to see his disciple again before death came. Paul's desire for fellowship with

Timothy reveals how important Christian fellowship was in Paul's judgment. Paul was an apostle who had received direct revelation from the Lord, and yet he realized the need for fellowship with other believers.

In addition to the fellowship, the following verses indicate other reasons why Paul was concerned that Timothy come before winter. Having expressed urgency for Timothy's coming, Paul wrote:

For Demas, having loved this present world, has deserted me and gone to Thessalonica; Crescens *has gone* to Galatia, Titus to Dalmatia (4:10).

One can almost sense the sadness in Paul's heart as he wrote concerning Demas. Paul had also mentioned Demas in Colossians 4:14 and Philemon 1:24, and from these verses it is apparent that Demas was respected by Paul and perhaps was even a co-laborer. Now he had forsaken Paul. Paul's distress over the departure of Demas was probably one reason he especially wanted to see Timothy at this time.

The word translated "deserted" is *egkataleipō*, which means "to abandon." But notice why Demas had abandoned Paul—"having loved this present world." The words "this present world" are literally "the now age." Demas had a change of affection; he was more concerned about what the world had to offer than he was about suffering for Christ and experiencing dangers and discomforts with Paul. This verse does not say that Demas had forsaken the Lord but that he had forsaken Paul in his time of need.

Paul also mentioned that Crescens had departed to Galatia and Titus to Dalmatia, but there is no indication that these men had also forsaken Paul. Rather, they were probably sent by Paul to these areas, for later he said that he sent Tychicus to Ephesus (v. 12).

The loneliness of Paul without these companions is indicated in the first phrase of the following verse:

Only Luke is with me. Pick up Mark and bring him with you, for he is useful to me for service (4:11).

In Colossians 4:14 Paul had referred to Luke as "the beloved physician." Paul's appreciation for Luke had doubtless become much greater, as now only he was with Paul. This also gives us a glimpse into the stability and faithfulness of Luke.

Having expressed his situation, Paul then instructed Timothy: "Pick up Mark and bring him with you." Mark was apparently serving in the same vicinity as Timothy, and Paul wanted Timothy to bring him when he came to Rome. Paul said concerning Mark: "For he is useful to me for service." Paul longed to have the very man brought to him whom he had once rejected. On the first missionary journey, Mark was a companion of Paul and Barnabas, but Mark turned back before the trip was completed. Later, when Paul and Barnabas were planning a second missionary tour, Barnabas wanted to take John Mark with them, but Paul absolutely refused because of the earlier incident (Acts 13:13; 15:36-39).

The indication is, however, that Paul and Mark had become co-laborers later (Col. 4:10; Philem. 1:24). But now Paul had special need of Mark, and he asked specifically that Timothy bring Mark with him. Paul's words concerning Mark are a reminder that even though a deep breach or clash develops between individuals, the relationship can be restored if both are willing to put Christ first. Paul did not say specifically why Mark would be useful to him in Rome, but some surmise that it was because Mark had been there previously and would have been acquainted with Rome and the Roman Christians.

Paul's opinion concerning Mark had greatly changed. He had considered Mark useless to take along on the second missionary tour, but now he had been a co-laborer for some time, and Paul wanted him to be brought to Rome, where he would be useful to him.

But Tychicus I have sent to Ephesus (4:12).
Although it appears from the words of this verse that Paul had already sent Tychicus before writing the letter, it was customary in the Greek language to use what is called an "epistolary aorist." It is so called because in the writing of epistles, or letters, the writer would sometimes take the viewpoint of the reader and express the thought in the aorist tense. Tychicus was probably the one who brought the letter to Timothy, so as Timothy read the letter he would see that Paul had sent Tychicus to Ephesus. Perhaps the reason for Paul's doing this was that Tychicus was to take the place of Timothy and Mark, who were to be leaving as soon as possible to visit Paul in Rome. Thus, Tychicus would be Paul's representative among the churches in that area, as Timothy had been earlier.

From Paul's first letter to Timothy it is apparent that Timothy's responsibility as Paul's representative was to see to it that the various church matters were conducted properly and that qualified men held leadership positions in the local assemblies.

Chapter 25–
Instructions for the
Trip

When you come bring the cloak which I left at Troas with Carpus, and the books, especially the parchments (4:13).

IN THIS VERSE, Paul referred to three things that he wanted Timothy to bring when he visited the older apostle in Rome—his cloak, his books and his parchments.

A cloak in Paul's day was a long, apparently sleeveless circular cape of heavy material that had an opening only at its center, for the wearer's head. The garment would be especially needed in cold weather, and because Paul was writing from a damp dungeon, he no doubt had in mind the coming winter months. This seems apparent from what he later told Timothy: "Make every effort to come before winter" (v. 21).

Although Paul's concern for his own physical comfort was on a far lower and more world-conscious level than the other more godly elements in his letter. It is not unspiritual, however, to give proper attention to physical needs. If anything, it is unspiritual for the believer not to give proper attention to the needs of his body—the temple of the Holy Spirit (1 Cor. 6:19). It is a false sense of spirituality for one to neglect his physical needs.

But Paul was concerned with more than just the physical, for he told Timothy to also bring "the books, especially the parchments." The word translated "books" is the plural form of *biblion* from which the word "Bible" is derived. The books to which Paul referred were probably papyrus sheets or rolls. This writing material was made from the papyrus plant. Strips of papyrus were pressed together and dried to make an inexpensive writing surface.

The word translated "parchments" is the plural form of *membranas,* from which the word "membrane" is derived. These parchments were animal skins and were more permanent as well as more costly than papyrus. Precisely what was included in the "books" and "parchments" that Paul wanted Timothy to bring to Rome has been the subject of much conjecture and debate. Several commentators consider the parchments to have been Old Testament portions which Paul wanted for study and meditation. Others suggest that these may even have included a record of his Roman citizenship that Paul needed in his trial before the imperial court. Still other Bible scholars agree that they were portions of the Old Testament Scriptures, but they differ as to why Paul wanted them. Rather than wanting them for study and meditation, some commentators suggest that he wanted them to show the court that what he was teaching was not an illegal religion. It was a religion as legal as that of the Jews, because he was using the same writings as his source. Whether Paul did or did not use these written materials in his appeals to the court, one can be sure that having any Old Testament portions would certainly have given the apostle considerate comfort and encouragement in this difficult ordeal.

Having asked Timothy to bring these things with him, Paul then mentioned an individual who had caused him much trouble:

Alexander the coppersmith did me much harm; the Lord repay him according to his deeds (4:14).

It is uncertain to whom Paul was referring. "Alexander" was a common name in Bible times, and thus it was necessary to use a qualifying phrase to tell which Alexander Paul meant. Paul identified him only as "the coppersmith," or metal worker. In his first letter to Timothy, Paul also referred to a man by the name of Alexander; "Among these are Hymenaeus and Alexander, whom I have handed over to Satan, so that they will be taught not to blaspheme" (1:20).

If this were the same Alexander Paul had mentioned in his earlier letter, he probably would have identified him more specifically than just as "the coppersmith." Knowing only his trade wasn't much identification, but even this broad designation would help Timothy to be on the alert for any metal worker by this name.

Paul said that this Alexander "did me much harm" but did not specify the wrong the coppersmith had committed. The following verses give a clue that perhaps in the trial itself Alexander had done harm to Paul and to the cause of Christ.

The word translated "did" is *endeiknumi*, meaning "to show," or "to demonstrate." This word indicates the thought that Alexander may have attempted to expose Paul before the imperial court. To damage Paul's defense in the eyes of the judges would be equal to damaging the cause of Christianity in the Roman empire.

Paul added concerning Alexander: "The Lord repay him according to his deeds." The word translated "repay" is *apodidōmi*, meaning "to give back" or, in this context, "to pay back." Some think that Paul was expressing a wish which evidenced personal vindictiveness. However, had that been the case, Paul probably would have used the optative mood to express a wish. Instead, he used the indicative mood to indicate a biblical principle for evildoing: "The Lord will repay him according to his deeds." So instead of personal vindictiveness, Paul was simply stating that God will have final victory over the forces of evil.

Although he was certain that God would eventually be victorious, Paul warned Timothy concerning Alexander:

Be on guard against him yourself, for he vigorously opposed our teaching (4:15).

Paul gave Timothy an explicit command: "Be on guard against him yourself." The word translated "against" is *phulassō*, meaning "to guard against," or "to look out for," and also "to avoid." Paul put this word in the middle voice, which indicates that the subject participates in the action. So this statement meant "keep yourself away from him." Paul saw nothing to be gained by encouraging Timothy to dialogue with Alexander, for Paul realized that no good would come out of such an encounter. Although the believer is to reason with others from the Scriptures, some people are entirely unreasonable, and nothing can be gained from such a contact. In fact, the cause of Christianity might even be harmed.

Paul referred to the manner in which Alexander had done him evil in his phrase: "For he vigorously opposed our teaching." Paul may have referred to Alexander's opposition to the Christian message he proclaimed or to Paul's own defense at his trial. But an attack on either the message or the defense would have affected the other. This also indicates that Alexander's form of persecution of Paul was not physical but mental. The reason Alexander's opposition was so serious was apparently because of its potential in hindering the gospel. A person with such obvious ill will was to be avoided.

Chapter 26- Paul's First Defense

At my first defense no one supported me, but all deserted me; may it not be counted against them (4:16).

THE GREEK WORD translated "defense" is *apologia*, meaning "answer" in the sense of "defense" or "reply." From this Greek word "apologetics" is derived. The words "first defense" can refer either to Paul's first imprisonment a few years earlier or to the first stage in the trial he was now undergoing. Most likely, Paul was referring to a preliminary hearing in his present trial, where the charge was read and where he had opportunity to give an initial statement. Thus, his *apologia* was an answer to the indictment lodged against him.

In his first defense, Paul said, "no one supported me, but all deserted me." From the word *paraginomai*, meaning "stood," we get a glimpse into the Roman legal system. This word was used technically to refer to assistants whom the Roman courts allowed to speak in behalf of the accused. It doesn't necessarily mean that there were no Christian friends with Paul, such as Luke, but only that those who were qualified to stand before the court and speak in his behalf refused to do so. Understandably, it was a dangerous matter to take Paul's position before the Roman government. Christianity was regarded as an illegal religion in the Roman Empire. Therefore, it would have involved risking one's own life to speak in defense of Paul, who was known throughout the empire as a chief spokesman of Christianity.

Instead of defending him, those who were qualified to speak for Paul "deserted" him. Paul used the same word here as he used in referring to Demas (4:10). These friends, like Demas, had deserted him in his time of need.

Despite their failure to aid him, Paul said, "May it not be counted against them." What an evidence of the grace of God in a person's life! Just as Stephen forgave those who were stoning him to death (Acts 6), Paul forgave those who refused to act as his advocates, thereby hastening his own day of execution. Only one who has a deep sense of God's grace in the forgiveness of sins could exercise such grace toward others. As Paul reflected about those who refused to stand by him in the time of crisis, he thought of the One who never left his side:

But the Lord stood with me and strengthened me, so that through me the proclamation might be fully accomplished, and that all the Gentiles might hear; and I was rescued out of the lion's mouth (4:17).

Paul knew that even though no qualified person would argue his case before the judge, the Lord had not forsaken him. Not only did the Lord influence the judge—as indicated by the fact that Paul's trial had been temporarily delayed for further investigation—but the Lord also gave Paul boldness to proclaim the gospel. The Lord stood with Paul and "strengthened" him. He empowered Paul to effectively present his own case before the judge.

Paul indicated the intended result of the Lord's strengthening: "So that through me the proclamation might be fully accomplished, and that all the Gentiles might hear." The trial was Paul's opportunity to present the claims of Christ before the highest earthly tribunal and before the crowd who would have gathered for such court proceedings.

It isn't clear from the text what Paul meant by his reference to "all the Gentiles." Probably he was referring to all the Gentiles who had gathered to witness his trial. Also, Paul may have realized that his trial in the capital of the Roman Empire would actually publicize the cause of Christianity to the entire Gentile world. In either case, this was a strategic time in Paul's personal life and in the history of Christianity as he was called upon to defend the cause he represented.

To his statements concerning the enabling of the Lord and the intended purpose, Paul added: "And I was rescued out of the lion's mouth." There is no definite article with "lion" in the Greek text; therefore, it should read "a lion" rather than "the lion."

Some have suggested that Paul was referring to Nero, Satan or the lions in the arena to whom Christians were thrown. However, if Paul was referring to either Nero or Satan he would probably have used the definite article with the word. And as a Roman citizen, Paul would not have been cast to the lions in the arena. It is better to understand this as expressing deliverance from extreme danger, as is evident in Psalm 22:21.

The Lord rescued Paul at the preliminary stage of his trial in that no definite sentence was issued by the court at that time. As Paul thought about this deliverance, he wrote:

The Lord will rescue me from every evil deed, and will bring me safely to His heavenly kingdom; to Him *be* the glory forever and ever. Amen (4:18).

Although the Lord had delivered Paul physically during the first stage of his trial, Paul fully expected to be condemned by the judge, as indicated by his words in verse 6: "For I am already being poured out as a drink offering, and the time of my departure has come." But Paul did not fear death; he viewed it as a deliverance from every evil work in the world and a transference to the "heavenly kingdom." To the Philippians, Paul had earlier written: "For to me, to live is Christ and to die is gain" (1:21).

Paul's word for "evil" (*ponēros*) in 2 Timothy 4:18 refers to evil that is in active opposition to good. Paul viewed this world as the arena of conflict between good and evil. Though a judge might make a decision to end his life, Paul knew he would be preserved by God for His heavenly kingdom. Evil might seem to triumph over good for a time, but ultimately God will be vindicated and good will reign supreme.

His thoughts of God and His kingdom caused Paul to break into a doxology: "To Him be the glory forever and ever. Amen." Since his conversion, Paul purposed to glorify the Lord in his daily living. He had not always been successful, and he was intensely aware that there was nothing good in his old nature (Rom. 7:18). But Paul realized that God was ultimately going to bring glory to Himself and that this glory would last throughout all eternity. The Greek expression *eis tous aiōnas tōn aiōnon* is literally "unto the ages of the ages" and was the Greek way of saying "forever and ever."

Having made this statement as a doxology to God, Paul concluded with "Amen." The Greek word translated "Amen" is a transliteration of the Hebrew word for "truth." Paul's use of this word reveals that, even in the face of death, he had full assurance of faith in God.

Chapter 27– Paul's Last Words

Greet Prisca and Aquila, and the household of Onesiphorus (4:19).

AS PAUL CONCLUDED his letter to Timothy, he wanted Timothy to pass on his greeting to some friends. He first mentioned "Prisca and Aquila." The husband-and-wife team had greatly endeared themselves to Paul as co-laborers in the gospel. When Paul wrote to the Christians in Rome, he also sent greetings to this Christian couple and described them as those "who for my life risked their own necks, to whom not only do I give thanks, but also all the churches of the Gentiles (Rom. 16:4).

From the greetings Paul communicated through Timothy, it is evident that Prisca (or Priscilla, as she is sometimes known) and Aquila were in the area of Ephesus, having left Rome perhaps because of the persecution in that area. That this husband-and-wife team had meant much to Paul is also evidenced by the fact that he placed them first in his list to be greeted—both in Romans 16 and here in 2 Timothy 4.

Paul also wanted Timothy to pass on his greetings to "the household of Onesiphorus." This is the same household Paul mentioned at the beginning of his letter (1:16-18). Onesiphorus had greatly encouraged Paul during his Roman imprisonment, and Paul was concerned that the members of his household be given a special greeting.

Erastus remained at Corinth, but Trophimus I left sick at Miletus (4:20).

Background is not given concerning Erastus and Trophimus, but the fact that Paul alluded to them indicated that he thought Timothy would wonder concerning the whereabouts of these two men. What Paul said about Trophimus is especially interesting in regard to physical healing. Although the apostles had the divine ability to heal people, it is evident from this statement that healing did not always take place. Imagine—a companion of the Apostle Paul who was left at Miletus, sick! Such an incident coincides with 2 Corinthians 12:7-10 (referring to Paul) and with 1 Peter 1:6-7 (referring to believers in general) and indicates that it is not always God's will to heal.

Having sent greetings through Timothy, and having given information about Erastus and Trophimus, Paul now instructed Timothy:

Make every effort to come before winter. Eubulus greets you, also Pudens and Linus and Claudia and all the brethren (4:21).

Paul here repeated his request that Timothy come to him. In this same chapter Paul said, "Make every effort to come to me soon" (v. 9). In verse 21 he emphasized the element of urgency by saying, "Come before winter." Not only would travel be difficult, if not impossible, for Timothy in winter, but it is also likely that Paul wanted his cloak (v. 13) before winter set in.

Having stressed the urgency of Timothy's coming to him, Paul then communicated greetings to Timothy from the four friends—Eubulus, Pudens, Linus and Claudia. These four are not mentioned elsewhere in the New Testament. Paul also communicated greetings from "all the brethren." He had said earlier, "Only Luke is with me" (v. 11). Therefore, it is likely that "all the brethren" of verse 21 are all those with whom

Paul was in contact through Luke.

The Lord be with your spirit. Grace be with you (4:22).

The pronouns of this last verse make a distinction. In the first sentence, "your" is singular, showing that Paul was addressing only Timothy. In the last sentence, "you" is plural, showing that Paul was addressing all readers of the letter.

Paul ended his letter on the same keynote with which he began it—"grace." This word was more than just a greeting to Paul, for he was intensely aware that he deserved the judgment of God; and yet He evidenced grace to him through the Lord Jesus Christ. Having trusted Christ as Savior on the road to Damascus, Paul had been delivered from condemnation, and after that, the word "grace" was always foremost in his thinking.

Second Timothy is the last letter we have from the Apostle Paul. How thankful believers can be that God preserved this giant of the faith until he could pen this letter which has been of great encouragement to the Church throughout the centuries.

Acknowledgments

MANY PEOPLE NEED to be thanked for bringing *Treasures from the Original,* back into print.

The one who first gave me the love for the Greek New Testament was the late Dr. Terry Hulbert. I am indebted to him and many others for giving me a love for the entire Word of God.

Thanks goes to Back to the Bible that first published this in 1975 with the title *Gems from the Original.*

Thanks go to the many local churches where it was my privilege to teach 2 Timothy in Bible conferences.

A special thanks goes to Renee Fisher for her enthusiasm and help in preparing this book for publication on Amazon.

About the Author

Dr. Harold J. Berry is a former professor of Bible and Greek at Grace University of Omaha. He served for many years as personal assistant to Theodore H. Epp, founder of Back to the Bible. Dr. Berry holds a Master of Theology degree from Dallas Theological Seminary and a Doctor of Divinity from Grace University.

www.ingramcontent.com/pod-product-compliance
Lightning Source LLC
Chambersburg PA
CBHW032009040426

42448CB00006B/552